Writing for Newspapers and News Services

WRITING
FOR
NEWSPAPERS
AND
NEWS SERVICES

Howard C. Heyn

THE ASSOCIATED PRESS

&

Warren J. Brier

UNIVERSITY OF MONTANA

Funk & Wagnalls   *New York*

Foreword

There is probably no one in the world who would not like to be able to write clearly and convincingly so that his ideas can be completely understood. This is particularly important today, not only for journalists but for everyone—businessman, educator, scientist—who must present his ideas to the public.

Despite this need, however, many brilliant students are reaching college and even being graduated without an adequate understanding of basic writing principles.

The authors of this book, while aiming particularly at those who aspire to careers in journalism, have written a simple, direct, and comprehensive program, which, if followed, can make a better writer of anyone. Of course, it is of primary interest and of greatest use to students in journalism schools or to those in other schools who might want to follow a career in journalism. It is also useful to those students studying for other careers who nevertheless must write theses or term papers.

Most difficulties in achieving a readable style, the authors contend, are related to simple faults in composition, among them long, awkward sentences in which it is easy to misplace clauses and phrases; wordiness, the bane of all good editors; obscurity; and failure to include all the essential points of the story.

The necessity for a direct style, a thoughtful choice of words, and the development of interest through organization as well as by sharp observation are also considered.

8571

The book includes individual sections on how to phrase leads, make the most effective use of elements of color and mood, and handle feature material. Chapters are devoted to obituaries, which get only passing attention in most texts, and to the technical variations in writing and editing for newspapers, news services, and news broadcasters—subjects often ignored in the literature of journalism.

No one can teach a person all of the things that make an interesting journalist, but this book will help its readers to solve basic writing problems. And the authors are to be complimented for their direct and comprehensive approach to writing problems.

WES GALLAGHER
General Manager
The Associated Press

Contents

FOREWORD by Wes Gallagher, General Manager,
The Associated Press   v

I   *The Scope of the Book*   3

II   *The Nature of Readability*   9

III   *Areas for Improvement—Style*   27

IV   *Areas for Improvement—Interest and Attitude*   54

V   *Descriptive Writing—The Quest for Color*   80

VI   *Starting the News Story—The Lead*   101

VII   *Obituaries: The Delicate Description of Life and Death*   131

VIII   *Feature Favorites*   147

IX   *Newspaper, News Service, Radio-TV News Writing: How They Differ*   165

X   *The Newspaperman and the Language*   191

INDEX   205

*Writing for Newspapers
and News Services*

I

The Scope of the Book

A few years ago, the authors—both employed by a wire service—
observed a young woman begin her first job as a professional
writer. Her credentials were impressive: she was a Phi Beta
Kappa, a graduate of a well-known school of journalism, and a
former editor of her university's student newspaper. Moreover,
she was attractive, eager, neat, and personable. But she was unable to write at the level demanded by a major wire service bureau. She was dismissed after a probationary period.

The young woman's failure raised this question: Why should a
person apparently so geared for success fail in her first professional writing job? The answer is not clearcut, though the authors
now believe she did not adequately understand the fundamentals
of good writing and she had not been exposed in her schooling to
the kind of writing required by newspapers and wire service bureaus that insist on craftsmanship of the highest caliber. She

was not prepared to join an organization in which newsmen must work fast, yet weigh each word, each sentence, and each paragraph against the possibility that the opposition is telling the story more clearly, more colorfully, more dramatically.

Her situation, not at all uncommon, was simply this: what she had done so well in the classroom she was unable to do under the pressures of actual performance in earning a living. Furthermore, her plight had nothing to do with her sex; males are equally prone to failure under similar circumstances.

Perhaps the young woman could have succeeded on a small or medium-sized daily, though many such newspapers also demand a high degree of professionalism. Actually, she did do well in another type of journalism in which the emphasis was almost wholly on reporting, not writing.

Let us say now, for purposes of argument, that instead of taking a nonwriting job the young woman in question had joined a small daily paper on leaving the wire service and that she had succeeded there because the more leisurely pace provided an opportunity for personal coaching by experienced superiors. This supplementary assistance to a scholarly journalism graduate amounts to nothing less than *retraining*. Among experienced editors it is a widely held belief that, in utilizing journalism graduates professionally, a certain amount of retraining is inescapable. Quite obviously, this view does not enhance the image of college journalism schools. But the need exists nonetheless. You can, for example, write headlines for four years in the classroom and then run into trouble with the style and letter-counts prescribed by the copydesk on your first job. This is an expectable adjustment, and it is certainly not insurmountable. Far more serious among the shortcomings of many newly graduated news writers is the discovery that sentences and paragraphs and stories do not assemble so smoothly and so easily under the requirements of speed, space, and reality as they did under the conditions set up by a teacher.

What, then, is the best way to prepare for a career in the commercial news media? Start from scratch, as a copy boy, and work up? Some make it that way, just as some self-made men in other fields ultimately achieve great wealth. Their scarcity, however, does not recommend this system.

We doubt that working newsmen ever attended a professional seminar without hearing from the floor this question: "What, in your opinion, is the best way to improve schools of journalism?" And we doubt that any seminar ever lacked at least one reply like this: "Teach less journalism. Teach more political science, history, economics, etc."

There is a certain amount of truth in this view, enough to make it popular. But the authors of this book certainly do not go all the way with this argument. We do not believe that good schools of journalism have failed. We do feel, however, that many of the not-so-good departments have erred in *emphasis*. These incline too heavily toward the academic point of view. The practical aspects of a career craft have, too often, been neglected. In many curricula, for example, newspaper ethics, editorial writing, and the history of journalism (in forms that no longer exist) are required undergraduate subjects. How soon will the journalism student write an editorial for a metropolitan—or any other—paper? When will he face the need, as editor-in-chief, to formulate policy, or to assess relationships between press and society?

As electives, or graduate courses, such subjects have their place. Time allowing, the student should be exposed to all possible facets of an activity in which he expects to earn a livelihood. But not at the expense of sufficient emphasis on more immediate, more basic elements.

Of these, clear and correct composition is perhaps the most important. In all too many cases, unfortunately, it is assumed that the student reaches the college level well grounded in grammar and syntax, whereas the truth is that both elementary and high schools have failed in this respect. The unhappy proof lies in the fact that both authors (and myriad editors) have seen far too many beginners with *graduate* degrees in journalism who could not properly line up the clauses of an ordinary sentence and who could not even make the verb tenses agree. These are writers?

Retraining, then, frequently becomes imperative at a very late date and at a point much too high in the scale of instruction. It is indeed sad that college time should be taken away from the refinements of education in any field, but there it is. And, if retraining is necessary, it should take place on the campus, not in the city room.

The young woman's experience and others like it strengthened the authors' belief that a need existed for a book that describes not only the elements of basic writing but the techniques of sharp, dynamic news writing. The advanced techniques, of course, depend on a thorough understanding of the basic elements, for the polished writer never achieves such stature by taking syntactical shortcuts.

This book endeavors to describe both the elementary principles of news writing and the methods employed by veterans who have earned the admiration of their colleagues. The book is based, in part, on the belief that a person trained to write for newspapers or wire services can shift with little discomfort to writing jobs in radio and television, public relations, and even to posts with technical publications and magazines. It does not, however, pretend to be all things to all students; the young person interested in broadcast journalism or publicity work will profit immeasurably from textbooks prepared especially for those fields.

The format differs markedly from those of other books about news writing and reporting. An entire chapter, for example, is devoted to the preparation of obituaries, a subject slighted by some journalism texts. Yet the young newsman is likely to write obituaries during his first day on the job—and he may be writing them still on the day of his retirement.

Two chapters describe in detail possible areas for improvement in news writing. One discusses style, the other interest and attitude.

Another chapter deals in depth with the news-story lead. The reason for such an extended discussion: most beginning writers find the lead unusually hard to write, primarily because they do not fully understand the function of the opening sentence and because they have not examined closely enough the leads written by veteran newsmen. This chapter presents both the fundamentals and the refinements, with examples by experienced writers.

The book is distinctive also in the number of examples used to support, or illustrate, discussions about news writing. The student is advised to peruse the examples with extreme care, for they show how talented writers have solved prose problems that he will encounter many times.

This is not a book about reporting. Several superb texts already exist on that phase of journalism. This book does not tell you how to ask questions or how to mark your copy for the printer. It mentions but does not stress the organization of the newsroom or the function of the telegraph editor. It does not point out the difference between libel per se and libel per quod. That information should be presented in the classroom and has been presented often in other books. But this book will help you to improve your writing—it will point you in the right direction as a professional writer.

Over the years much has been said about the inadequacies and outright sins of the daily press. Much of that criticism has come from the victims of the press—real or fancied—and not nearly enough from those who, as members of the profession, have been far more likely to know what they were talking about. The newspaper business has its shortcomings, to be sure. So has the law; otherwise, legislatures and courts would not be nearly so busy revising and interpreting statutes. But inasmuch as this is not a book dedicated to the clinical dissection of news media, its authors firmly decline to compound the controversy, except insofar as it relates to the competence of the people who gather, write, and edit news. We do believe that large areas for improvement are strikingly evident, and that students of journalism—for their own future protection and success—should know what those areas are.

Moreover, the authors believe, as William P. Crozier so aptly put it, that "it is unjust that journalism should be judged by its slums and tenements and literature by its fine mansions and noble monuments." The critic of American journalism too often pretends that a tabloid or two and a few crime-and-sex-oriented dailies represent this nation's press. They do not.

Finally, the authors contend that unless a writer loves the language—unless he has a true feeling for words and unless he learns to admire brilliant writing while deploring sloppy prose—he never will become a professional journalist in the truest sense. Nor will he be able to escape a feeling of drudgery that accompanies any job when the practitioner discontinues his efforts to improve as a craftsman and stops what should be a lifetime study of the tools and techniques with which he works.

II

The Nature of Readability

In the Beginning was the Word

Of all the great sociological forces in life none is more powerful than communication. And none, except pure science, has embodied more amazing changes in less time.

Within the span of a single generation the methods and the media by which we convey information, ideas, and opinions have developed at a rate which is almost frightening.

The printed word of the daily newspaper, the spoken word of radio, the picture and speech of television—endlessly and almost immediately active—affect in one way or another every human every minute of every twenty-four hours.

The impact of this bombardment with which our eyes and our ears are constantly assailed has, in fact, given birth to a new force —semantics—and a new set of problems. The meaning of words, spoken or written, has been recognized at last as one of the great controversies in our complex way of life. Small wonder, then, that semanticists see rising from this communicative flood a twentieth-century breed of monsters, one of which is propaganda.

What we say, what we mean. Are they the same? Only too rarely. They embody, nonetheless, the very essence of the journalist's job: to bring together, as closely as is humanly possible, the word and the fact or concept which the word represents.

In facing this task the writer—newspaper man or broadcaster—has today not only the intellectual responsibility of transmitting truth (which has always existed) but also a problem in the element of time. The need is now. Life runs fast.

It may be difficult now to imagine that in the days of the carrier pigeon, one lifetime ago, newspaper publishing and newspaper reading were rather leisurely pursuits. Nobody expected to hear or see in print the report of a distant happening within a matter of hours. The average semi-serious reader in those days spent the evening with his paper, even saved it for closer reading the next day. If a story was complex, he took pride in figuring it out—in "reading between the lines." The more important, the more grave the occurrence, the longer and heavier he expected the story to be; anything else he would have considered frivolous.

But today's reader-viewer-listener is beset by multiple demands upon his time and attention. We must make news reading and listening as easy and quick as accuracy will allow. The breakfast table reader, the homebound bus rider, has time and interest for the first paragraph. If that snares him, he probably will read on. If it doesn't hold his attention or if it isn't clear, his eye will stray, just as his ear will close automatically to the ambiguous sentence spoken on his car radio.

A complicated sentence may be accurate, grammatical, and, with study, completely intelligible. But the hurried reader and listener will not grasp it. It will do no good to explain in a later sentence, or to say it again; you have already lost your audience. He simply hasn't the time to be bored or confused.

It is well known that most of the big news stories (and some of the very best) are produced under adverse circumstances, just as great events take place in settings reflecting tragedy, danger, or threat to national security. It is also true that news often is read, or heard, under adverse conditions. At least we as news disseminators must take these conditions into account. The language of news must invariably be translatable, in the human mind, upon first reading or first hearing. When the normal reader or listener fails to absorb immediately and fully what we have to tell him, we must blame the writer.

Speed is responsible. Speed has engendered virtually all of the changes in news production, just as it has created the reader-listener problem of assimilating information under conditions far less than ideal. Speed in news transmission, speed in printing, speed in pictorial reproduction, speed in delivery. Almost everything about the business has changed, radically and dramatically, except the words. One might almost say that electronics has outdistanced linguistics.

Actually there has been change, too, in the language of news, but more is indicated. That is, far more attention is imperative today in the choice and arrangement of words for rapid-fire delivery to a rushing civilization.

Phrased inexpertly or pretentiously, facts can have the effect of lies, or half-truths. They can misinform by confusion, just as they can noninform by omission.

This, then, in summary, is the role the reporter must play in the modern scene: he must tell what happened in terms the average literate person will grasp at once. Every lead and every subsequent paragraph must be clear, true, incisive, and interesting, so that the reader-listener will be impelled to stay with our story. We must not delay him with wordiness, confound him with imperfect sentence structure, or discourage him with dull, technical phraseology. We must give him the drama and color that come from judicious selection of detail, delivered with relaxed, conversational technique. Above all, we must not overfeed him by trying to force everything into one sentence.

Readability

It is quite feasible to be even more specific in our approach to the writer-reader-listener relationship. News writing reaches its highest (most translatable) readability when it develops its message ACCURATELY, CLEARLY, QUICKLY, COMPLETELY, and INTERESTINGLY.

Let us look briefly now at these elements of readability, about which a great deal will be said, in one form or another, throughout this book: Accuracy is directly related to fact, of course. But news is not all facts. News is quoted opinion, explanation, sometimes interpretation, several other things. Thus, accuracy is not only the fact but the right word in the right order to convey the fact.

Clarity relies almost completely on simplicity. Complicated sentence construction, awkward alignment of clauses and phrases, unexplained technical or esoteric terms are confusing and, in the ultimate, noninformative.

Brevity, which corresponds to quickness, is a universal virtue. In news writing it has a special value, as we have already seen in the foregoing snapshot of hurried, harried humanity. We have to be quick to catch our reader-listener. Brevity not only lures him, it also impresses him because it gives our message added power. Except in rare instances, the longer the sentence the weaker its impact.

Completeness means simply that the story answers all the pertinent questions readers and listeners will be certain to ask.

Interest is many things in news writing. Primarily, it is the human element, the personal touch that makes the reader-listener feel related to the occurrence in some way, most often emotionally. His attention is held; he wants all the story.

Achieving Readability: An Obstacle Course

In pursuing these elements of readability we will have to (a) dodge a series of roadblocks; (b) understand the structure of the simple sentence. These conditions are one and the same. However, negative factors will be considered in the following discussion because, oddly enough, it is frequently easier to see the wrong way, and avoid it, than it is to delineate the right way. Here, then, are the roadblocks:

Long cluttered sentences. The worst of these appear at the beginning of the story—in the lead—where they repel the reader before he can get to the news. But they also are real obstacles anywhere in a story.

Notice that the following example takes the reader all the way from Kentucky to Washington and back to Arkansas in search of its message:

> A demonstration in front of a desegregated Kentucky school was broken up by police Wednesday on the eve of the U.S. Supreme Court's momentous special session on the speed of the integration at Little Rock High School.

Such a sentence can be guaranteed to discourage readers in Kentucky, Washington, Arkansas—and everywhere else.

General wordiness. Overwriting has two counts against it: it makes dull reading and it steals space. Nothing saps a story more completely than verbal dysentery; nothing strains an editor's patience more severely than unnecessary words. Most rambling sentences never would get into print if we always wrote the way we should edit.

General wordiness takes three forms:

(a) Loose construction. Consider the following:

The police officer accompanied the two to Utah last week inasmuch as it was felt that young Melvin could be of use in helping to locate or identify the killer.

We can say the same thing this way:

The policeman accompanied them to Utah last week, hoping Melvin could locate the killer.

We now have 14 words, against 30 words before; at this rate we would be wasting 160 words in 10 paragraphs. Incidentally, a thousand useless words will waste considerably more than a column of newspaper space and will kill twenty minutes of transmission time on a news service teletype wire.

(b) Redundancy is another manifestation of wordiness. It occurs by word, by phrase, and even by sentence. How many times have you seen, in the body of a news story, a sentence which repeats, almost word for word, a statement which appeared in the lead? Even more common are such phrases as the following (in which the needless words are capitalized): "ABOUT several months old"; "Continued ON"; "SHORT snub-nosed revolver." You will recall many more.

Most often redundancy is the product of the writer's haste or failure to think. But sometimes it springs from a mistaken notion that saying something twice is twice as effective as saying it once. We encounter this frequently in the use of direct quotes:

Former Gov. Goodwin J. Knight and his wife arrived Wednesday with no plans except for a little golf and a lot of relaxation.
"I haven't any plans," Knight told a news conference. "I want to take a rest for about a month in Palm Springs and play some golf."

Repetition is the best of all ways to waste words; it delays the reader for absolutely no reason whatever.

(c) Needless detail. This third form of wordiness is more a matter of judgment than a matter of phrasing. Which details are really pertinent to the story? The decision must precede the writing. In other words, determining *what not to write* is a prime function in good reporting. We can't tell everything. If we could, reporting would be vastly simpler, for it is easier (with a minimum of training) to gather information than it is to project it on paper or in an acceptable verbal account. Even granted unlimited space and time, a story containing all the details of an occurrence, however momentous, seldom would be read or heard in entirety.

Choice of detail depends upon audience as well as upon time and space. That which might interest one set of readers very easily will bore, or delay, another audience. Wire service editors, for example, find poor choice of detail a common failing among "stringers" (correspondents) in outlying areas. The stringer, who probably works for a local weekly, by force of habit will include in his wire service offering a blow-by-blow padding of trivial facts which could not conceivably concern any reader in another state, or even another fairly distant community. "The car collided with a BUREAU OF LAND MANAGEMENT fire truck AT THE INTERSECTION OF JOHNSTON ROAD AND TOWNSEND LANE eight miles southwest of town" contains, in the capitalized phrases, two examples of detail possibly pertinent for one audience but purely superfluous for another.

No audience at all needs lesser descriptive detail wholly unrelated to the circumstances of an event:

> She was shot to death in her father-in-law's RANCH STYLE home a mile from here.

Many news stories are heavy with such pointless facts, collected and tossed in by reporters overly anxious to demonstrate how observant they are.

It is strangely true that we all use more words the faster we write. It is also unhappily true that news accounts excessively laden with trivial detail very often lack important facts. A news story widely printed at the time it occurred told about three children who died by fire in an apartment, the only door of which had been nailed shut. The reporter devoted two paragraphs to the number and placement of nails which held the planks blocking the door. But he failed to say WHY the door had been nailed shut.

The above account was a news agency story, and it should be emphasized here and now that wire services are by no means immune to any of the faults which will be cited throughout this text.

Obscurity and complexity are probably the chief roadblocks to readability, because the source from which they spring is the source of nearly all other basic writing problems: the failure to construct a proper sentence. It seems incredible that college students, and professional newsmen as well, should lack a foundation of common grammar, yet the evidence is all around us in the newspaper and on the air. Far too many fail to construct proper sentences because they do not understand sentence elements and their correct arrangement. A great deal will be said on that point later in this chapter.

The long, complex sentence composed of poorly aligned clauses and phrases is the most prolific breeder of obscurity and confusion. An example:

> Bob Lemon entered the game in the third inning to hit a single between a walk and a ground out that provided the Tribe's only run it scored off Johnny Kuchs until the final inning when Rocky Colavito smashed his eleventh home run of the season after Mickey Vernon's single.

On the other hand, even a sentence which is brief and quite simple can be obscure if it fails to cover all the aspects of situation:

> Wallace denied a motion for continuance of a hearing sought by U.S. District Attorney Phil Crew.

The obscurity: Did Crew seek the hearing or merely the continuance? No one could possibly tell from that sentence.

Along with complicated and inexact sentence structure, a common cause of confusion and obscurity is the use of unexplained technical terms and the hifalutin phraseology of government handouts.

This untranslated medical diagnosis is guaranteed to stop our reader-listener dead in his tracks:

John T. Godfrey, 37, the nation's second ranking World War II flying ace, died in his home today of AMYOTROPHIC LATERAL SCLEROSIS.

A detailed discussion of the roadblock created by technical, legal, and governmental language will be undertaken in the section on style in chapter III.

Failure to answer all the questions which the reader obviously will ask is, quite simply, failure in our initial purpose: to inform. This roadblock likewise will be considered more deeply under style in the next chapter because, like governmentese, it concerns content rather than sentence structure. Reference to both is made in passing here, however, inasmuch as they are definite factors affecting readability. "Amyotrophic lateral sclerosis" is one example, and here is another: a nicely composed Christmas story which failed to see the light of day reported that a crippled child home from the hospital (but going back after the holidays) was thrilled most by the gift of a shiny, new bicycle. Can he ride it? Will he some day? The story didn't even speculate.

It is time now to return to the second requirement in the pursuit of readability. You will recall the earlier statement that to make the reader-listener's task as easy as possible we must (a) avoid roadblocks and (b) understand the structure of the sentence. Within this second requisite lies the key to the journalistic writing process.

The Sentence. "Keep your sentences simple."

In the classroom, or in the city room, this usually is the first instruction the novice newsman gets. And so it should be. If he gets it in the classroom first, he is ahead of the game.

The well-cast simple sentence is the news writer's greatest safeguard against ambiguous, wasteful, hard-to-read, and often inaccurate composition.

So just what is a simple sentence?

Technically a simple sentence has one clause. It can be highly effective if its message is equally simple and if it is used intermittently. ("He said, 'Get out!' ") But the grammarian's simple sentence isn't very versatile. It won't always say as much as we need to say in a single statement. A sequence of one-clause sentences is as monotonous as a mile of fence posts viewed from a train window.

Such writing is neither adequate for the reporter nor suitable for the reader. Far more appropriate, in direct communication, is the familiar structure which lies somewhere between the abrupt one-clause assertion and the extended, heavily balanced "literary" sentence whose many parts must be studied before their full import can be translated in the mind of the reader.

This compromise might be called the "simplified" sentence. It has more than one clause; it may be compound or complex in the sense that it comprises direct clauses, or both direct and indirect clauses, along with sundry modifying phrases.

But for maximum readability it *must not be too long*. Its clauses and phrases *must be arranged in exact order*.

These key conditions—length and order—are directly responsible for the speed and accuracy with which the reader receives the message. Misaligned clauses will confuse and delay him, perhaps cause him to misinterpret the meaning of the sentence.

All of us have encountered sentences which we have had to rearrange mentally as we read them. All of the necessary words were there, but in the wrong order.

Excessive length—too many clauses and phrases—will produce the same effect, even if all the sentence parts are properly arranged; the reader will have been given too much detail to assimilate clearly, quickly, and accurately.

Well, how long is too long?

You can find out, in nearly all cases, by applying the following two-question test to sentences of your own or those written by others:

1. Read the sentence quickly and only once. Did you fail to relate instantly the principal subject and predicate? If you did fail, they are too far apart. Shorten the distance between them by removing one or more of the clauses or phrases (for use in a later sentence).

2. Did you, in the same single reading, fail to absorb at once the effects which all of the qualifying and modifying words have upon subject and predicate? If you did fail, the sentence is too long.

Although designed primarily as a yardstick for *length*, the two-question test quite frequently can be applied to *order* as well.

Let us look more closely at these essentials of the simplified sentence. The parts of the following sentence need to be rearranged for maximum clarity and effectiveness:

A law designed to force the American Red Cross to label blood plasma shipped into Louisiana according to race goes into effect July 30.

Rather obviously, blood plasma isn't *shipped* according to race, yet that is what the sentence says. Also rather obviously most readers will be able to figure out that this is not what the sentence means. Even so the sentence wastes time and effort. The reader will have to *work harder* to determine exactly what the sentence does mean. The true message has been delayed.

Let's shuffle the units in the sentence and deal them out in a new order:

After July 29, blood plasma shipped into Louisiana by the Red Cross must be labeled according to race.

It will be noted that, in revamping this sentence, we have not reduced its message at all, but we have avoided these roadblocks: obscurity, wordiness, and haphazard cluttering of phrases.

It is quite possible, of course, to confuse the reader-listener or otherwise impede him with a sentence which is relatively well ordered. This happens when we offer him too much detail at once (apply question 2 qualifier-modifier test). In such instances it is necessary, for quick comprehension, to reduce the message. Study for a moment the following example:

> The chief prosecution witness at the trial of the accused murderer of a prominent druggist hanged himself in his jail cell today.

The writer of this statement cannot justifiably be accused of mixing his phrases; they are in reasonable order. But witness, accused, and victim are so closely linked that the reader must hesitate momentarily to sort them out. He even may have to read the sentence again. The distance between subject and predicate is too great for immediate assimilation of all that we are being told; we have to *stop and think* if we are to determine accurately just who hanged himself. In fact, two (and possibly three) sentences have been strung together with prepositional baling wire.

The way around this barrier is to concentrate upon the *main portion of the message* in our initial sentence:

> The state's chief witness in a murder trial hanged himself in jail today.

The remainder of the news—the lesser details of identification —follows in another sentence:

> Felix von Gleed was to have testified against the man accused of slaying a prominent druggist last September 21. Von Gleed's body was found . . .

By making two sentences out of one in the above example, we reduced the message of each to enhance clarity and to speed the reader on his way. In the next example we will also reduce the message, in a sense, but without resorting to two or more sentences. This is possible because much of the statement's so-called information is purely superfluous:

> The biennial general council of Congregational Christian Churches, in session here, today sent a telegram to House Speaker Sam Rayburn and House minority leaders urging full support of the administration's foreign aid program, now before Congress.

It should be noted first that this sentence is even more orderly than the preceding example. Nothing in its arrangement will mislead the reader-listener; it is clear, accurate—and windy. It exemplifies the roadblock of sheer wordiness, and thus it takes too long to read in relation to what little it says. But rewriting isn't necessary; editing will correct its loose construction:

> The biennial general council of Congregational Christian Churches endorsed the administration's foreign aid program today.

What have we eliminated and why?

The council is "in session here." That's obvious.

Councillors sent a telegram. The reader can assume this, if indeed he cares in this instance how their action was made known.

They addressed it to both majority and minority leaders—that is, to Congress as a whole. So what need is there to specify?

"Urging the full support of" is the long way to say they recommended it.

"Now before Congress." As obvious as "in session here."

Wordage of the sentence has been reduced from thirty-six to fifteen—more than half. On the basis of the original sentence, it would take twice as long to read the paper if all stories were comparably overwritten. Equally important, the revised version is far more lucid.

It is an unfortunate fact that Americans, as a whole, are highly critical of the way their language is spoken by other nationalities newly arrived in this country. They frequently cite the "fractured" English of foreigners without seeming to realize that their own speech, if not exactly broken, is rather badly dislocated. As we pursue our analysis of the well-integrated, simplified sentence we will find that one of the most frequently dislocated parts of speech is the verb. Because verbs convey action, their placement in the sentence is important, as you will see in the following example:

> Mary must take the Pasteur treatment unless the black dog that bit her while she fed birds in the meadow behind her grandmother's farmhouse twelve miles south of here is found by the health department.

The principal verb in the conditional clause is not encountered until the end of the sentence. But when we place it where it belongs the sentence at least makes sense, with subject and predicate in proximity:

> Mary must take the Pasteur treatment unless authorities *can find* the black dog that bit her while she fed birds in the meadow behind her grandmother's farmhouse, twelve miles south of here.

We are making progress, but we still do not have a truly *simplified* sentence because we are trying to say too many things at once. Again we should divide the message into two sentences:

> Mary must take the Pasteur treatment unless authorities can find the black dog that bit her. She was feeding birds in the meadow behind her grandmother's farmhouse, twelve miles south of here.

Here is a really elaborate example of the same syntactical situation:

> A New Orleans dressmaker who allegedly teamed up with a self-styled private investigator to defraud a group of persons by telling them that a billion-dollar settlement was imminent in their claims as heirs to Trinity Church property at Wall Street and Broadway was arrested today by postal inspectors in her Park Avenue suite.

The bones beneath this obese assertion, if you can uncover them, are: "A DRESSMAKER WAS ARRESTED for fraud." Building on this skeleton, we get:

> A New Orleans dressmaker was arrested today in her Park Avenue suite by postal inspectors who charged that she teamed up with a self-styled private investigator to defraud a group of persons by telling them a billion-dollar settlement was imminent in their claims as heirs to Trinity Church property at Wall Street and Broadway.

It reads, yes. The clauses and phrases are in line. With effort on the reader's part, they make sense. But a *simplified* sentence?

Hardly. Its complex message should be broken up. You might get by with two sentences, but three would be better. This time, you try making the division.

The best *simplified* sentences convey their meaning without fuss or fuzziness. While order and length are paramount, other qualities enhance this delivery process:

1. Active verb forms are the fastest vehicles. Direct sentences are the easiest to read, and active verbs travel the direct route between writer and reader. Passive verb forms lengthen the sentence, making the reader work harder, and may even confuse him.

2. Wherever possible, active verbs should also be colorful verbs. These command attention, sustain interest.

3. Tense and number must conform, for reasons of clarity as well as grammar.

4. Subjects and objects must be immediately identifiable. In other words, watch those pronouns!

This is what is meant by the passive approach:

> His call appeared to be a revival of what was known in past administrations as the Good Neighbor Policy in America.

Actively expressed, this is all that the sentence says:

> His appeal *recalled* the Good Neighbor Policy of past administrations.

The next example isn't passive in construction but it is equally indirect:

> One pilot parachuted to safety but the other fought for control of his plane before also bailing out after the two jet fighters collided.

The first and most important action—the motivating action— comes at the end of the sentence: the planes collided. Rearrange the clauses to feature the primary action and the sentence has far more direct impact, as well as greater clarity:

After the two jet fighters collided, one pilot parachuted to safety but the other tried to regain control of his plane before he too bailed out.

The following is both passive and indirect:

A top-ranking rocket AFD space weapons expert *coupled the disclosure of his resignation* from the Air Force today with a blast at the senior scientists upon whom the services rely for technological advice.

Writing of this sort—and there is a lot of it in Washington—is as curvy as a mountain road. Straightened out, the sentence means:

A top-level Air Force space weapons expert blasted civilian scientists today and said he had resigned.

Colorful verbs are not necessarily unusual verbs. They are, however, appropriate verbs always, and the following examples show that the best of them are also active:

A thirteen-inch cloudburst *drowned* nine persons, *swept away* homes and buildings, *ripped out* bridges and *flattened* crops in southwest Iowa today.
Live broken electrical wires *curled* in the street like snakes about *to strike.*

Tense and number are violated with remarkable frequency by the hasty writer:

The Soviet Union *turned over* the bodies of six crewmen recovered from the wreckage but *has denied* any knowledge of the accident. (Tense)

The couple *departed* on a brief honeymoon after the ceremony and *plan* to give a reception next month. (Tense)

A young society couple yesterday *was* divorced quietly, in marked contrast to the furor that surrounded *their* wedding. (Number)

To whom in a sentence does a pronoun refer? This variety of confusion is easily avoidable by use of the proper name:

He decided to run for mayor after Blank failed to win election to the U.S. Senate in November and then announced *he* would seek a fourth term in city hall.

Claude Watson testified that a 1943 check of Beck's financial affairs showed that *he* and Frank Brewster borrowed $80,000.

In other words, "Who he?"

Summary

In charting a course toward the highest level of readability, it is almost impossible to overstate the importance of constructing sentences in simple, orderly fashion. Failure to do so accounts for most of the ambiguity—and a great many other faults as well—which we find so easily in present-day news writing. But proper structure cannot be expected of writers who do not understand sentence elements.

The examples offered in this chapter demonstrate (a) how an awkward arrangement of clauses and phrases can impair the clarity and even the accuracy of what we say; (b) how even a passably well-aligned sentence may delay the reader-listener, confuse him, or kill his interest if it contains a volume of detail sufficient for two or three sentences; (c) how sheer wordiness, although well ordered, can impede and irritate him for no valid reason; (d) how the greatest impact can be achieved by direct statements employing active, colorful verbs; (e) how easily we can leave our audience bewildered and uninformed by errors of tense and number and by inexplicit pronominal identification of subjects and objects.

Before closing this chapter a word of reassurance is in order for those who may have misconstrued—or taken too literally—the emphasis which has been placed on the so-called simplified sentence. Some, quite possibly, may have concluded from this discussion that all long, balanced sentences are bad. Such a notion would be completely erroneous.

It is not our intent to decry any type of sentence, so long as it is fashioned by a seasoned craftsman along lines related to his purpose. Literature is full of rolling, periodic constructions embodying beauty, rhythm, and decorative form. Aside from their affective value they may also be utilitarian on occasion, as the semanticist S. I. Hayakawa demonstrated so cleverly by using a periodic sentence to *define* a periodic sentence:

"A periodic sentence is one in which the completion of the thought is, for the sake of the slight dramatic effect that can be produced by keeping the reader in suspense for a while, delayed."

This can be effective even in news writing, now and then. The point of decision rests upon appropriateness. Thus it must be apparent that most of the time the simpler syntax best serves the needs of journalism, wherein rapid writing and quick comprehension are indispensable.

III

Areas for Improvement— Style

Newspaper writing is more than a technical craft. It is also a state of mind.

Grammatical competence is not enough; the good journalist is constantly *aware* that he is communicating. The pursuit of this purpose leads him to seek the appropriate word, the smooth phrase, the concise sentence, the coherent paragraph, the well-ordered article.

"Consciousness of writing" sounds like an intangible factor. It isn't. This awareness is just as vital to the communicative process as is syntax. Its development, therefore, is a very practical part of journalistic training.

The novelist frequently writes for himself; he says things in the manner he prefers, for personal reasons. The true reporter must never permit such self-indulgence; in every sentence he writes he must remember the reader he is pledged to inform.

A news story may be perfect grammatically and rhetorically, yet defective in every other way related to communication. It can be just as misleading, ambiguous, newsless, or dull as if its sentence structure were wholly wrong.

In short, *how* we say something must be completely correlated with what we have to convey, so that we will deliver our message to the reader-listener accurately, clearly, and quickly. Correct grammar is merely the prerequisite. Communication is the goal.

There are three broad areas in which today's news writing should be improved. Two apply to the process of preparing the news account: *style* and *interest*. The third concerns the writer himself: his *attitude* toward his task.

Style

How we say it is a process involving many refinements upon the grammatically correct simple sentence. Taken together, these refinements constitute *style*. And such *style* as we develop individually depends largely upon the degree to which we understand, and employ, these extra qualities. We will consider under style a number of things to aim for and a number of things to avoid.

It is easy to find statements which, in syntax at least, meet all the basic requirements of the simplified sentence, yet do not constitute the *best* way to say what we have to say. Style, for our purposes, therefore concerns taste, judgment, order, and content, as well as grammatical accuracy. An appealing flow of smooth, crisp, informative simple sentences requires planning before writing. Extra thought is the price of this extra quality.

The elements of style to be discussed here may be listed as follows:

(A) Factual order; (B) choice of words; (C) separation of ideas; (D) attribution and identification; (E) completeness.

(A) *Factual order.* This is the state we achieve when we say first things *first*. We noted in the preceding chapter that the most effective sentence presents its clauses and phrases in proper alignment for clarity and quick comprehension. We must arrange our fact messages in precisely the same pattern.

Failure to say first things first has a serious effect upon the delivery of news. We will call this failure *inversion*, and you will see a lot of it in the daily press. You won't hear so much of it in radio and television newscasts because we are far less likely to invert when we talk. Broadcast news is conversationally written.

The late Wolcott Gibbs of *New Yorker* fame, parodying *Time* magazine, summed up inversion this way: "Backward ran the sentences until reeled the mind." And Roy Copperud, the *Editor and Publisher* columnist, called inversion "linguistic smog."

The first thing the reader wants to know is *what happened*. Inversion delays the news. In doing so it may also delay the points of interest which will keep the reader attentive. An inverted sentence, backing into the news, characterizes this lead:

> An Atlanta businessman who joined two anti-Negro, anti-Jewish groups and turned over information to the FBI today associated a man on trial for dynamiting the Jewish Temple with race-hating John Kasper.

Rearranged with first things first, the sentence becomes newsworthy:

> A man on trial for dynamiting the Jewish Temple was linked with race-hating John Kasper by an undercover agent today.

Lesser detail, which led off the original sentence, then takes its proper place in a second sentence:

> The witness was an Atlanta businessman who joined two anti-Negro, anti-Jewish groups and turned over information to the FBI.

The prime news is buried again in this inverted sentence:

> Harry Tenebaum, St. Louis investment banker, told today of conversations with members of the Federal Communications Commission (FCC) but denied engaging in behind-the-scenes activity to win a television channel award.

The news comes first when the lead is turned around and split into three sentences:

An investment banker denied today that he acted behind the scenes to get a television channel.

Harry Tenebaum of St. Louis told the House Oversight Committee that he talked to members of the Federal Communications Commission. But he swore he couldn't remember who they were.

The final sentence above had been in the second paragraph of the story, where it was out of context.

Avoiding inversion is, to a large extent, a matter of maintaining the reportorial point of view. A simple hypothetical situation will illustrate:

You are walking along a beach in the fog. A man, running toward shore on a breakwater, looms into view. He shouts to you, "A ship just sank out there! How do we get the Coast Guard?"

You both hurry to a phone booth while he tells you what else he saw: a tanker, its helmsman obviously blinded by fog, steered into the end of the sea wall. Almost immediately the ship broke in two. Awestruck, the man on the breakwater watched the vessel's halves disappear within minutes. Then he ran for help.

One newspaper account you read next morning was introduced this way:

An eyewitness running out of the fog on Redondo Breakwater brought the first report today of a shipwreck.

A certain element of drama is apparent in this approach, to be sure. But it emerges from the word picture of a frightened man racing along a breakwater in the fog. Fictionally, the approach has merit. Journalistically, the emphasis belongs on the ship and what happened to it. Only one word—and the very last word—is newsworthy.

The opposition newspaper reported the event properly:

A supertanker broke in two and sank today after smashing against Redondo Breakwater in blinding fog.

Inversion is often the product of hasty writing. In such cases the reporter may overlook, momentarily, an essential fact. Suddenly recalling it, he throws it in wherever he happens to be in the course of phrasing the sentence. Apparently just this happened in typing the following sentence:

Seven persons on beach outings waded into the surf for a boy caught in deep water today *and drowned.*

The reporter must not *write* faster than he *thinks.* He did so in this instance. Otherwise the news would have been placed where it belongs—at the top rather than at the bottom of the sentence:

Seven persons drowned in the surf today while trying to save a boy caught in deep water.

In producing the following example the writer was so preoccupied with a direct presidential quote that the news became an afterthought:

President Eisenhower brushed aside "whatever difficulties the Soviets may raise" to talks on a nuclear test suspension today and sped three scientists to Geneva.

He should have written:

President Eisenhower *sped three* scientists to Geneva today, brushing aside "whatever difficulties the Soviets may raise" to talks on nuclear test suspension.

Sometimes inversion generates sentences which are confusing or actually misleading, faults even more serious than burying the news. Example:

Ditson and Carlos Cisneros, 29, San Fernando watchmaker, whom the governor saved from execution, were convicted of slaying Robert Ward on November 6, 1959, near Castaic Junction.

Were both saved from execution or only the watchmaker? Who could tell? In precise factual order the sentence should be phrased:

Ditson and Carlos Cisneros, 29, San Fernando watchmaker, were convicted of slaying Robert Ward on November 6, 1959, but the governor saved Cisneros from execution.

This could be further improved by breaking the statement into two sentences: ". . . on November 6, 1959. The governor . . ."

The misconception that lodge affiliation influenced an appointment is implied in this example:

Long a member of the Masons, he became principal in 1959.

The factual order in this sentence certainly was not what the writer had in mind:

Kostadinoff was fined $800 and costs last March under a charge of transporting *liquor made by* Hancock County authorities. (*Springfield* [Ohio] *News*)

Participial phrasing, a writing gimmick popularized by flashier newspapers, is a prolific producer of inverted, indirect sentences. This technique can, on occasion, be quite effective when it hooks the reader with an active, colorful verb form. But it also embodies the weakness of subordinating the news. A return to our shipwreck example will show how:

Smashing against the Redondo Breakwater just offshore in a heavy fog early today, a *supertanker broke in two and sank* within minutes.

Furthermore, the participial introduction of a sentence can very easily induce a grammatical error known as a dangling modifier:

Ailing in recent years, Smith's literary output dropped to almost nothing by 1963.

Possibly Smith's writing was sick, but we doubt that the reporter intended to say so.

In most cases participal constructions lengthen sentences needlessly and, since they are indirect, they often turn out to be passive as well. In the latter case their usage lacks even the asset of verbal action to attract a reader. Here is such a weakened sentence:

He was ordered to face a hearing *for the slapping* of the school board president. (Active: ". . . for slapping the . . .")

The practice of participial and gerundial writing-in-reverse long has been a favored elegance among weekly newspaper writers, for reasons which are still obscure:

> *Filing* the complaint *was* Beverly Drum.

> *Taken* to a hospital after a rescue crew cut through the wreckage with acetylene torches *was* Joseph Dineen, 15.

(B) *Choice of words.* The second factor in this discussion of style calls for the same sense of precision that is demonstrated by proper factual order. Here again the hazard is haste—the hurried reporter is inclined to write faster than he thinks. The result is *inept phrasing.*

A single poorly chosen word or phrase can create an awkward sentence, even reverse the meaning. *The New York Times* specialist Hanson W. Baldwin unintentionally made himself appear the most arrogant of Harvardites when he included the phrase "but nevertheless" in the following sentence:

> Saito is an old man (75), a Yale alumnus, but nevertheless has a clear mind and is concise and direct.

The same error and the same effect:

> *Although* a native of Nebraska, Prof. Stone displays a fine command of the English language. (*Beloit* [Wisconsin] *College Round Table*)

Too often the result is downright ridiculous, as in this paragraph from an Erle Stanley Gardner novel (*Murder Up My Sleeve*):

> Malloy's fingers groped for his hat *brim,* removed it. "Glad to know you," he said.

Similarly absurd:

> Her message to struggling writers is, "If you want to write *badly* enough, you can." (*Evansville* [Indiana] *Courier & Journal*)

"Get" and "got" frequently get you into trouble, as in this sentence from the *Canarsie Courier:*

> Walter B—— added another rescue to his list when he swam out to *get a young woman in trouble* some thirty feet off the beach.

All verbs, in fact, have to be carefully chosen lest they make us say something silly:

> Howard Chandler Christy, the noted illustrator, *took* fifty-two mackerel fishing on the Viking II with Capt. Carl Forsberg, out of Freeport on Monday. (New York *Mirror*)

For some reason, accidents and acts of violence seem to breed inept phrasing:

> Miss Mamakos was revived by the Fire Rescue Squad, but was *otherwise* uninjured. (Washington *Post*)

> Heill was in improved condition after being shot in the lower back. (A bullet now and then is good for everybody?)

The one word "with" reverses the meaning of this sentence, since it makes the literal statement that the witnesses have needlessly given the cops a bad time:

> Witnesses accused the police *with* unnecessary roughness.

In a great many instances choice of the wrong word is the result of sheer ignorance. For many years reporters have been counseled to choose terms which are familiar to the average reader, but—deplorably enough—this is not always an adequate safeguard. Even words which nearly everyone has heard are misused repeatedly. Familiar as they may sound, their true meanings may not be equally well known. The proof was offered by the reporter who wrote this sentence:

> The CAA has *instigated* a program of civil-military coordination.

"Instigated" has a derogatory connotation. The writer meant "instituted" (and "begun" would have been simpler).

A completely antithetical notion of a word's meaning "got in the way of communication" between writer and reader in this sentence:

> *Semantics* got in the way of communication during the special meeting of the Board of Governors of the La Canada Unified School District Thursday night at the Foothill Intermediate School, causing the session to be prolonged until almost midnight. (*Montrose* [California] *Ledger*)

This television announcer, reporting an international gymnastics competition, simply didn't know what he was talking about:

> The European nations have such a *vast nucleus* to draw from.

The following is quoted from an editorial in the American Newspaper Guild's official publication, *The Guild Reporter*, (wherein one would expect a sharper understanding of such words as "between"):

> There was unprecedented solidarity *between* the seven unions that jointly struck the two Honolulu papers.

As if to emphasize a poor choice, the editor italicized the word. "Among" might have served his purpose more ably, or he could have phrased the sentence: "The *solidarity* of the seven unions . . . was unprecedented." He did much better in the next paragraph:

> Equally important, if less dramatic, there was corresponding solidarity *within* each of the seven unions.

Colloquialisms and words with double meanings turn up continually in sentences which are ineptly phrased:

> A fire tonight *chewed out* the interior of Balsam Inn, a noted restaurant south of town.

> He likes *for* dogs to be kept inside.

> James Thomas, twenty-one-year-old Negro laborer, pleaded innocent today to murdering Dr. Gaylord Henry, who was found *clobbered to death* in his animal clinic last year.

The *figure of speech*—about which more will be said in a succeeding chapter—is fertile ground for ineptitudes. Here is an excellent way to gum up the machinery:

> He [Westbrook Pegler] has been a cog in the newspaper grind, though an *ever-growing cog*, since 1916. (Washington *Post*)

This must have been a highly irritating silence:

> Seventeen hundred people might have been *painted on their seats*, so still were they. (New York *World-Telegram*)

And even the hardworking farmers are overdeveloped in the Midwest:

> It was the more placid summer of the Middle States, buxom as a *big-bosomed farmer's* daughter. (From *Along These Streets*, by Struthers Burt)

A nonexistent verb from Outer Space:

> The Teamsters Union aimed another dove at the CIO but the federation *potshotted* the bird on sight.

Clichés, and *trite expressions* in general, are ever-growing evidence of failure to devote sufficient attention to choice of words. Clichés, regrettably, will always be with us; we have to live with them. Inevitably they will creep into rapid writing. The important thing is to keep them in check. Like any necessary evil, they should be used in moderation.

Not all clichés are bad. Some have become so common that they are part of the idiom, automatically as acceptable as are impersonal pronouns and such nouns as "today," "tomorrow," "yes," and "no." No one appears to be irritated by such expressions as "It's a lovely morning," "very well, thank you," "I'll be seeing you," although these are hackneyed indeed. Yet we are all weary of "weary firefighters" and we wince when we see, for the thousandth time, "withering fire," "violence flared," "pumped two bullets into his abdomen," "beefed-up campaign," or "a wild chase through rush-hour traffic at speeds exceeding 100 m.p.h."

Most reporters who will take the time to think a little will find that they possess sufficient imagination to avoid such phrasing as "the Senate today *heads into* . . . ," "a fifth day of debate on the *bitterly contested* bill," or "*delicate* operation," to name but a few.

Critics of sports pages never fail to lambaste the plethora of clichés to be found there. They are, however, wasting their time. In sports writing, apparently, there is no such thing as the over-use of such verbs as "blast," "drive," "smash," and "spark," or such phrases as "came from behind." No amount of punishment will kill them. They are so much a part of today's sports pages that, in a sense, they have ceased to be clichés and have become fixtures, like pronouns and articles, imbued with unlimited mileage potential. Consistency compels us to counsel that a little imagination should be shown by sports writers, too—but, frankly, we are not hopeful.

Careless selection of words also is responsible for misused verb forms ("an accident that *saw* the top of the car sheared off"); prepositional wordiness ("imprisonment of up to ten years"), and misphrased approximations. The latter are highly common: "*some sixty-six* pounds of luggage," "*about forty-four* members," "*approximately twenty-eight* of the eighty-seven victims." Approximations should be just that: round numbers. Used with semi-exact totals such as sixty-six, forty-four, or twenty-eight, approximations become ludicrous.

The writer of this sentence was more concerned with approximation than with news:

> *Approximately* an hour after he had returned from an evening meeting *around midnight* Thursday, William R. Hamer of 9748 Cabanas Avenue in Tujunga died of an apparent heart attack in his home.

The *pun* is produced by a very deliberate choice of words, but whether the choice is good or bad is a moot point. Pun lovers (and there are a lot of them among newspaper readers) probably regarded these as very good sentences:

A herd shot around the world arrived at Rome today for the papal pastures.

Bruce was permitted to buy Petunia—a black and white skunk without a scent to her frame. (From a story about a deodorized Christmas present)

Uncontestably a poor choice, however, is the language of most handouts. This gabble is based upon highly generalized terms, almost all of them abstractions, and has come to be known as gobbledegook, or—in Washington and other capitals—government-ese. Space exploration and other fields of advanced science in the atomic age have contributed plentifully, as we shall see later in this chapter.

The newsman's job is to *translate* the expert's gobbledegook, not to adopt it. Abstract phrases *sound* important yet unfortunately say next to nothing intelligible. "Significant relationships"; "since *over-all policy* was *brought into focus*"—such is the high-flown verbiage against which the semanticists launch their most powerful linguistic rockets.

Governmentese is the highest (or lowest?) form of abstract writing. A farmer's "overage on his allotment" means nothing more than his excess or surplus. And why did a wire service reporter write "an electrical malfunction probably stymied the shot" when he could have said that something as simple as a broken wire probably ruined the launching? That is what he—and the missile experts—meant.

Here are some examples of governmentese from Washington dispatches:

. . . under mandate to achieve conformity.

The delay could not be predicated on opposition to desegregation.

The sustention of the principle is all the more important . . .

. . . finalize a program for federally impacted school areas.

Washingtonese also is peppered with such phrases and terms as "upward adjustment," "expedited basis," "phase-out," "reported out," and "mark up" (a bill). *"Domestic disappearance* of soybean oil" means there isn't any. And a $5 daily expense account for policemen was reported as "a tax deductible subsistence allowance."

Ray Crowley, for many years news editor of the Associated Press bureau in Washington, summed up governmentese succinctly:

"No true bureaucrat will 'put the lights out' if he can possibly 'terminate the illumination.' "

The lingo of the lawmakers is, naturally, echoed in the press release. But long before the handout became an accepted—although somewhat ominous—factor in news writing, courtroom copy was heavily clouded by legal smog. Judicial proceedings were reported in the argot of one attorney addressing another. Deplorably, they still are, in a great many instances, to the bewilderment of millions whose formal education ended at the eighth grade or earlier, and whose only consistent sources of information are the daily press, radio, and television. Radio and TV announcers always have been smarter than newspaper men in avoiding technical language. It is something of a mystery why Latin phrases and lengthy reviews of complicated juridical maneuvers continue to characterize courtroom reporting for newspapers, sometimes to a degree approaching the absurd. Even those readers capable of comprehending it are forced to conclude that the writer is concerned primarily with displaying his own erudition.

Sometimes quoted in English derivations, more often in Latin, such words and phrases as *quit claim, demurrer, true bill, injunction, fieri facias, non obstante verdicto, equity, mandamus, depositions, torts, pro confesso, replevin, common law* are familiar to millions who haven't the vaguest idea what they mean. An integration story from Montgomery, Alabama, referred to "a request for a writ of coram nobis" and to "a petition for habeas corpus" in the same sentence. Neither was explained.

Legalisms are almost always unnecessary. In a very few instances a technical dispute between counsel and judge may be sig-

nificant to the story, and perhaps then the Latin must be included.
But an explanation must follow. In normal instances, however, the
translation alone is sufficient:

> Justice MacBride accepted the petition of County Counsel
> Robert Jones as amicus curiae, on a point of law.

> The petition of County Counsel Robert Jones as friend of the
> court was accepted by Justice MacBride. Jones' brief was offered
> as an aid to the court in determining a relevant point of law.

Thus, in the second instance, the reporter writes what was
meant, not necessarily what was said by the lawyer or legal doc-
ument.

Commonly seen in both civil and criminal actions is the plea of
"nolo contendere." Too seldom is it explained, and, when it is, too
often the definition is inaccurate. The person who pleads nolo
contendere is telling the court that he does not contest the charge
made against him (or the allegation in the civil suit.) In other
words, he is not pleading innocent and he is not pleading guilty,
neither agreeing nor disagreeing with the plaintiff. He is placing
his case or his fate in the hands of the court, on the basis of evidence. Yet quite frequently in criminal proceedings the reporter's
translation of nolo contendere gives the impression of guilt. Thus
it is much simpler—and much more fair—to forget the legalism
entirely and to state merely that the defendant declined to profess
either guilt or innocence upon his arraignment.

Equally common in the courtroom idiom is "et al.," which literally means "and others." In practical usage it connotes others associated with the principal parties, such as partners, shareholders,
or subsidiary organizations. In countless news stories "et al." turns
up, unexplained, confusingly tacked onto an otherwise intelligible
sentence. Why not just say, instead, "and others"? The writer
should have done so in this case:

> Don Hurd, secretary-treasurer of the International Typograph-
> ical Union, has been ordered to testify in Colorado Springs Thurs-
> day in the $2,412,000 antitrust action of the Scott Publishing Co.,
> Inc., of Kennewish against the Columbia Basin Publishers, et al.

The reporter made a mess of the following sentence because he used "preferred," in the legal sense, instead of the familiar verb "brought":

> Magistrate Alfred M. Lindau reserved decision for two weeks yesterday in the case of Harry Donenfeld, president of Merwill Publications, Inc., who was indicted some time ago on charges of publishing *obscenity preferred by John S. Sumner*. (New York *Herald Tribune*)

Paradoxically, the same reporters who are remiss in translating legalisms are, quite as often, guilty of oversimplification in recording criminal situations inside and outside courtrooms.

For example, police *accusations* frequently are confused with *charges*—sometimes with libelous result. A lead may say the suspect is "*charged* with stripping off her clothes and attacking her." In the first place, there is no such charge as "stripping off her clothes." This is an *accusation*. The *charge* in such a case would be assault, which would apply also to the subsequent act of "attacking" her. There happen to be libelous implications in this lead, as well, depending upon the suspect's intent: if he were merely angry with her, the act of stripping off her clothing could be simple assault or even disorderly conduct, misdemeanors punishable by fine or nominal county jail sentence. If he intended to kill her, or do "great bodily harm," the assault charge could be a felony carrying a penitentiary term. Similarly, "attacking her" could be a misdemeanor assault if he only slapped her, or a felonious assault if he molested her sexually.

The facts in the case cited were that the suspect, motivated solely by a desire to embarrass his victim, disrobed her in public and then "attacked" her by scratching her face when he pulled down her elaborate coiffure—a case of simple assault for which he served thirty days in jail. Thus the lead was potentially libelous, in that it implied a far more serious moral act.

Accusations may or may not be detailed in the *charge*, depending upon varying legal procedures of the several states. The point to remember is that accusations and charges are not one and the same. As a safeguard against libel it is imperative that the reporter differentiate clearly between charges and the accusations they entail and that he follow the complaint exactly in doing so.

One writer who "charged" a man with stabbing his wife in the neck (an accusation taken from the police blotter) got the story back from his city editor with a memo asking him to select the *charge* from this list: simple assault, assault with a deadly weapon, assault with intent to commit great bodily harm, assault with intent to kill, attempted murder, attempted manslaughter (voluntary).

Even so, it is remarkably common to read a crime story in which the actual *charge* never appears—only the accusation. Newspapers are the worst offenders; wire services, even at the risk of being beaten one by the other, will withhold such a story indefinitely, until the precise charge is determined. They do so because they are aware that libel laws differ greatly in the many states to which their reports are transmitted.

Among lovers of gobbledegook, none are more ardent than scientists—with the possible exception of the newspaper men who write about them and their work. It would be easy to name, among the staffs of large dailies, half a dozen science writers whose style has become so scholarly as to be virtually meaningless except to the scientists themselves. Thus they defeat their primary purpose of translating for average and sub-average readers the technical language of experts whose activities are highly significant in the news of this space-atomic age. So important is the scientific field in our daily life that even six supersophisticated reporters are far too many. How they retain their assignments is hard to explain; they should be writing for trade papers. In some cases, at least, the answer is that their editors are a little in awe of them (and poorer editors for it). On smaller dailies the average reporter is ill equipped to handle this kind of information and can use in his stories only the terminology he gets from his scientific sources. The result is technical phrasing which, for most of us, obliterates all meaning. Example:

It is no longer sufficient, Diercks said, to scale geographic co-ordinates from the rectangular grid of a topographic map.

During one news writing study conducted by the Associated Press, researchers found within a single week six stories containing unadorned references to "ion rockets." Finally came a seventh story, devoted exclusively to ion rockets, that did include the much-needed explanatory sentence: "Such vehicles use electrically charged gases for thrust."

Some explanations, on the other hand, are worse than none. One writer who chose to use the term "Igor camera" compounded confusion by adding this definition:

> An Igor camera is an intercept ground optical recorder, including a Mitchell high-speed cinechronograph through a 96-inch focal length lens at F6.3 on black and white 35-mm. motion picture film at a speed of sixty frames per minute.

Technical terms directly related to science (macromolecule, photosynthesis, dynamics) are hard enough to deal with, but the experts associated with government projects manage to complicate matters even further, by "labelizing" (Hardtack Series, Ranger 6 Program, Project Echo). And reporters endeavoring to save words by omitting descriptive or explanatory sentences are prone to pick up these handles. There are literally hundreds of them, one as meaningless as another to thousands of reader-listeners. If you use them, you will have to identify them. If you identify them, they will lose any possible value as shortcut devices.

We cannot blame the scientist for creating his own idiom any more than we can blame the newspaper man for developing his. Jargon—in the laboratory, in the city room, in court, in Washington, in business—is acceptable and even necessary to rapid conversation among colleagues. It becomes a fault and a problem only when communication crosses from one field into another. Perhaps unfortunately for him, the newsman must span many territories, and more often than not he must provide his own bridges if there is to be any communication among the innumerable, widely different areas of activity that comprise contemporary life and its news-hungry audience.

It is at this point that the press agent becomes a valuable assistant, whatever his commercial or otherwise selfish motives may be. His handout or his counsel, in our currently complex way of life, cannot be scorned categorically if he is an information specialist as well as a press agent in his field. It is up to the reporter, of course, to separate valid information from pure puffery. But in steadily increasing numbers today's public relations men are helpful intermediaries as well as promoters.

Science is only beginning to realize the need for such liaison with journalism. For too many years the scientist maintained his lofty station above the relatively unlettered masses. But science has outgrown its ivory tower and is rapidly infiltrating the realm of big business. Some link between the abstract and the practical has become imperative as well as expedient.

One branch, however—medicine—remains aloof, to its own detriment. Here public relations is still in its infancy. The majority of physicians, particularly specialists, not only expect the average reader to be ignorant of medical matters but also seem unwilling to cooperate in the informative process. The newsman faces a difficult problem in medical writing, largely because he faces it alone. Medicine's legendary contempt for the daily press and other news media is equaled only by the average doctor's disinclination to help avoid those very errors of which he complains so loudly and so long. Such a position is particularly inconsistent with the vast public interest in health now prevailing among reader-listeners. To meet the demand for such information the reporter must become a student in the field. The extent to which he succeeds varies greatly. This is all too apparent in the daily press.

During a radio interview a professor of dentistry in the space of five minutes made three technical references that were extreme to the point of affectation. He did not bother to define his terms but, happily, the interviewer was able to interpolate explanations.

However, this wasted valuable air time the faculty man could have used in imparting additional information. His references, and their translations by the announcer, were:

> "There has been a causal relationship established between carbohydrates and caries." (Decoded: "Pastries have been linked directly to the cause of tooth decay." The dentist was talking about desserts.)
>
> "Audio-analgesia." (Decoded: "Background music piped into operating rooms.")
>
> "Toothpicks traumatize the gingeva." (Decoded: "Toothpicks injure the gums.")

Oversimplification of medical situations is rarer than failure to explain, but equally undesirable. When you don't know, it is unwise to speculate. A reporter who couldn't find out from the doctors just what was wrong with Billy Graham produced this somewhat contradictory and altogether ridiculous statement (second sentence):

> A spokesman for Mr. Graham said the evangelist's ailment definitely has been isolated by doctors. *The ailment could be described as serious in one respect, but it was not believed that Graham's condition was anything to become distressed about,* the spokesman said.

(C) *Separation of ideas.* Some newsmen simply cannot resist trying to tell the whole story—or as much as possible—all at once. This occupational ailment results in a number of writing faults. It is, for instance, a chief cause of the *sentence that contains two or more unrelated ideas:*

> In the tenth round Garcia, *who has a wife and five children in Dallas, Texas,* clobbered Barkus with a left hook.

More than a grammatical error is involved here. Those whose attention is unstable (and who isn't easily distracted these days?) can be derailed by such a sentence. Our minds are required to switch instantly from one topic to another, and the chances are we will have to reread the sentence or give up entirely. As was noted in an earlier chapter, *time* and *ease of comprehension* are vital factors in addressing newspaper readers and radio listeners.

Incompatible facts in the same sentence are like cats and dogs in the same basket. Yet those writers who never mistreat pets will torture readers willingly, in this fashion:

> After the murder Lowell Lee, *who plays the bassoon in the university band and who had been a top-grade student in high school,* then threw the guns into a river and drove back to his rooms.

A writer can lose his audience irretrievably with two or three sentences like this:

> Detective Watson, a sixty-five-year-old former railroad brakeman *who still holds a Brotherhood of Railway Trainmen Union card,* said Beck told him in 1943 that he always keeps $1,500 in cash on hand.

Listeners are equally vulnerable. A radio announcer reporting a football game told his audience:

> The pass was intended for Joe Jones, *whose wife gave birth to a daughter day before yesterday.*

The obvious correction is two sentences, although not necessarily in sequence. In fact, story organization probably would call for separation of the alien ideas within the story as well as within the single sentence. Lee's skill with the bassoon may be worthy of mention in that portion of the account which deals with his personality. But it doesn't belong in the narrative section that describes his actions in committing a murder.

Equally disassociated are the two parts of this sentence, the varying thought in which should be located in different parts of the story:

> Once a judge on the state's highest court, Seabury broke his hip three years ago.

The absurdity of such double statements is immediately apparent to the writer who takes the time to read back. And he must learn to do this mentally, as he writes, not with a pencil after he finishes the story.

A far more common problem, however, is entailed in rapidly written sentences containing two or more ideas which are, in a sense, related, yet not closely enough to keep the reader on the beam. Precise writers automatically will phrase two or three sentences in such cases. But even the veterans will resort deliberately to these loosely joined thought combinations within a single sentence. In most instances they do so for one of two reasons: they wish to avoid repeating attribution, which might be necessary if they broke a single sentence into two or three; they fear that, having broken it, one or more of the resulting sentences might be deleted by the desk. Their devious aim is to thwart the copyreader, by wrapping everything into one package. And indeed editors do sweat over such constructions in trying to reduce the wordage of a story.

Here is an example of a sentence containing ideas only partially related:

> Martin F. O'Donohue, monitor board chairman, has made it clear that the anti-racketeering group may get in the way of the monitors' cleanup efforts and, also, that reforms have not progressed enough in the 1½ million-member union to insure a fair and democratic convention.

Unhappily, the writer hasn't "made it clear," at all. The same fault is evident in this example:

> Returns from 165 of 212 precincts gave Karth 27,728 votes to 12,898 for Joseph Dillon, who had won three terms as St. Paul mayor with labor backing before coming to Arizona, and 6,806 for Mrs. Donald Decourcey, a member of the city council.

Even when related, the juxtaposition of certain facts can be unfortunate:

The court overrode the Charlottesville school board's districting plan, which put all Negro elementary pupils in Jefferson (Negro) School District and turned down a fervent plea for another year's delay in ordering desegregation of Lane High School.

Who turned down the fervent plea? The court? Or the school district, in formulating its districting plan?

The same sort of confusion results from the following sentence, even though its idea-facts are associated:

He said that when nuclear-powered cargo submarines come into being, the Arctic will be used as a route for fast commerce between the east and west, thanks to the deep water slot called the Barrow Sea Valley which leads into the Arctic Basin from the Chukchi Sea off Point Barrow.

(D) *Attribution and identification.* Facts have sources, and the working reporter learns very early that these sources must be named if his account is to be *honest, believable,* and *safe.*

Who said it? Who did it? Who says he did it? Every reader has the right to ask these questions. Every news writer holds the obligation to provide the answers.

The stated authority for actions and assertions is, of course, particularly important to stories containing controversial opinions, incomplete or doubtful information, specialized knowledge, or any material potentially harmful to someone.

Among myriad definitions of news, the most cynical is "anything that hurts" one or another of those involved in the occurrence. This is obviously an overstatement, but it does serve to point up the necessity for attribution, since so much of what we call news is concerned with unpleasant, often tragic, happenings.

The following three leads, appearing successively on a news agency wire, illustrate the trap a newsman can write himself into through failure to attribute *questionable* or *developing* facts:

FIRST LEAD

A huge KC97 refueling tanker with *six men aboard* crashed and burned at 2:03 P.M. today in a salt marsh off the Isle of Hope. *All six men* aboard perished in earth-shaking explosions attending the crash.

SECOND LEAD (Half an hour later)
A KC97 refueling tanker crashed and burned 10 miles south-
east of here today, killing *all ten* crewmen aboard.

NIGHT LEAD (Two hours later)
Eleven Air Force crewmen died today in the flaming crash of a
KC97 tanker.

Quite understandably, the exact number of victims was in
doubt for an extended period of time following the accident. The
figures used in the first and second leads were "true" insofar as
investigators had determined them at the time. But the reporter's
inexcusable failure to attribute them in both leads left his news
agency wholly responsible for the toll. Both leads turned out to be
wrong. The precise number, finally ascertained, was reported in
the night lead.

Even here the reporter failed to attribute, although now well
aware that he had twice transmitted erroneous information. But
the night lead had the saving grace of being *correct*. Only when
you are absolutely certain—as an eyewitness—that you are right
may you dare to drop attribution, but even then it is best to play it
safe.

The problem of the three leads is interesting from this additional aspect; the reporter cannot be accused of incompetence; he
accurately reported what he was told. Furthermore, no one misin-
formed him, nor did he misunderstand what was said. Yet two of
the three stories were inaccurate, merely because investigation of
the crash had not been completed. The reporter's chief transgres-
sion was his failure to protect himself by naming a source.

In a certain degree, however, he was also guilty of misleading
his readers because he did not include some such qualification as
"the Air Force said first reports indicated six . . ." or "investigators, still searching the wreckage, said 10 bodies had been recovered. . . ." This would have let the reader know that no one, including the reporter, was yet certain of the facts. And the Air
Force would have been the authority for his tentative accounts.

The writer's need to protect others as well as himself (and his paper) is abundantly evident in situations embodying the possibility of libel. Both of the following sentences are openly dangerous, because of the absence of attribution and qualification:

> A private secretary *confessed* today she tried to hire a professional *killer* to *murder* her employer's wife because *she was in love with her boss.*

> Mrs. Barbara Fox Singleday, her $203,000 inheritance *stolen* by a Nevada dude ranch cowboy now held by the FBI, returned to her husband today in suburban Kirkwood.

Here is an example of minimum but adequate attribution:

> An Air Force C47 transport carrying 19 persons crashed and burned on a takeoff attempt at nearby Elmendorf Air Force Base today. *The Air Force said* 12 of those on board died.

In this instance there was no need to clutter the first sentence; witnesses to the crash were numerous, and military records at once established the number on board. Only the number killed was questionable and, therefore, needed a stated source.

All good things can be overdone. Unnecessary attribution or identification produces a graceless sentence, hard to read and delaying to the reader:

> *The Federal Bureau of Investigation said* today it is *checking* a story of an *itinerant who said* he was in jail with a *man who claimed* involvement in the 1936 kidnaping of Charles Mattson at Tacoma.

The qualification above is so excessive that the message of the sentence is smothered. And this one is even worse:

> *The Air Force,* using *reports* from the *Air Force hospital* at Charleston, *released a report saying* the two pilots were in serious condition.

Identification is carried to an extreme in this one:

> The Redbirds hammered three Japanese pitchers, including *Pacific League rookie of the year submarine pitcher Tadashi Sugiura.*

Overly cautious reporters write dull copy—a weakness equal to that of slowing the reader's progress. Attribution is important to the extent that it provides adequate and suitable authority for what is written. Beyond that point it becomes a roadblock to readability.

There are occasions when it is permissible to withhold attribution until the next sentence. This is unwise in reporting criminal matters, but the procedure can be followed safely in smoothing such a statement as the following, wherein identification delays the news:

> The director of the State Division Against Discrimination today announced an agreement with the Veterans Administration barring GI loan approvals to builders who discriminate because of color or creed.

As rephrased:

> Builders who discriminate against race, color, or creed will be denied GI loan approvals. The State Division Against Discrimination made this known today in announcing an agreement with the Veterans Administration.

(E) *Completeness.* No reader will be happy with a detective novel that omits the solution of the crime. But newspapers sell unsolved mysteries nearly every day. These are the stories that *fail to answer essential questions.* They comprise a prime fault of the daily press; examples are amazingly easy to find, in papers large and small.

Reporter and editor share the blame. Some of these stories are incompletely written, others are complete but inefficiently cut. In either case the result is unsatisfying to the reader.

Questions remaining unanswered may relate to uncited facts, unexplained procedures, undefined terms. Any account offering such mysteries is worthless, however well it may be phrased.

This problem of "mysterious writing" was introduced, in very general terms, during the earlier discussion of roadblocks to readability. (See chapter II, p. 17.) The following illustrations elaborate that reference:

News wires once carried a story about a sheriff who cleverly used infrared film and flash bulb to trap a burglar by photography. Almost incredibly, the report did not tell us that an infrared flash cannot be seen by the naked eye, an optical fact unknown to hundreds of thousands of newspaper readers. Invisibility of the flash was the whole point of the sheriff's strategy. Consequently, the entire point of the story was lacking.

What is a quarter horse? One-fourth horse, three-fourths zebra? How often do the racing columns trouble to state, somewhere in the text, that a quarter horse is specifically bred to run an exceptionally fast quarter mile?

A story about an impending strike of television players said that programs were being pre-recorded. It didn't say how the actors were persuaded to do the very thing that would nullify their walkout.

A Florida paper reported the arrest of two brothers suspected of shooting the sheriff's father eighteen years earlier. The account included the motive for the old crime, but not a word explaining why, after all these years, the sheriff became suspicious of the brothers, who had spent their lives in the bailiwick.

Another story, recounting the capture of an armed couple, ran more than a hundred and fifty words before telling the reader why they were arrested—for shooting a policeman.

Where non-essential detail is involved, it is always better to avoid the question than to evade answering it. Example: A story which referred casually to "a *grapho-type* machine operator in Chrysler's automotive body division" didn't say what such a machine accomplishes. If "grapho-type" had been deleted, the question would not have arisen—and the story would have suffered not at all.

We noted a few pages back that scientific gobbledegook produces many mysteries, and that sometimes the so-called "answers" to these are as puzzling as the original jargon. In other words, the initial question in the stories cited merely had been replaced by another, and neither had been *answered* at all. The same error was produced by the writer of an atomic power story, in which he dutifully undertook to translate the phrase "homogeneous reactor-type plant." But, in doing so, he used the word "slurry," which he failed to define. For innumerable readers this canceled his effort entirely. (Slurry is a watery mixture—mud, cement, or some other substance.)

Particularly irritating to readers are unanswered questions occurring in reports of spectacular happenings or feats of skill and endurance. Example: a neatly phrased wire story from Yosemite National Park, California, described how three alpinists scaled the south face of El Capitan Mountain for the first time. Then it said three persons were on hand to greet them at the top. How did the welcoming committee get there? Very simply. But not until several subscribing newspapers complained did the news service provide a supplemental dispatch containing the obvious explanation: the welcomers had climbed the relatively easy trail on the *north* face.

It is hard to understand how professional newsmen, presumably trained observers, could overlook or ignore factors so basic to the information process. Yet it must be admitted, sadly, that too often they do.

IV

Areas for Improvement— Interest and Attitude

Interest

Style, interest, and the writer's attitude were cited in the preceding chapter as the journalistic areas showing the greatest need for improvement. Our discussion has reached the second of these.

Interest is not solely dependent upon fascinating subject matter. Story organization has a great deal to do with it. Both aspects will be discussed, since it is obvious that even the most emotional of occurrences can lose impact in the telling if the writer assembles his material ineptly.

As we have seen, informing the reader is the primary purpose of the press. But boring him in the process defeats that purpose. Thus, transmitting information cannot be the only goal. If it were, it would be far easier to fill the newspaper with texts and transcripts of stenographic or taped reports. Minimal training would be required for such a procedure, yet how many people would read such accounts?

Charles A. Dana once said "the invariable law" of the newspaper is to be interesting. "The reporter," he added, "must give his story in such a way that you know he feels its qualities and events, and is interested in them."

In other words, the reporter must know how to choose the significant details.

The newspaper scanner who is wearied by a tedious account merely will turn his attention to another story, another page, another section, searching not only for facts but for stimulation. Pure sensation is not the answer, but all of us have seen too much that is drably recorded. Producing a successful newspaper entails a constant fight against dullness.

Why is the element of interest so important in news writing? Dr. Rudolf Flesch says the average newspaper reader's attention is inclined to wander because he has only limited knowledge of a great many subjects. No doubt this is true, but if we can't make a satisfactory newspaper of stenographic reports neither can we fashion one solely of material which titillates the subscribers—unless we abandon the informative purpose. We must, therefore, feed the reader the facts about topics of which he is semi-ignorant, and we must also offer these in a manner that seizes, and holds, his attention.

What *is* interesting in a spoken or written account? Almost anything which evokes an emotional response in the listener or reader.

The role of the writer is cast here. A few readers may have experienced what the reporter is recounting. But the writer is certain to be addressing a multitude of others to whom "nothing ever happens." In either case he must induce a *reaction* if readers and listeners of every category are to be satisfied with what he writes.

Cartoonist Al Capp has said that the emotional responses most appealing to the public are love, death, and power. These elements appear again and again in "Li'l Abner." Their effect is universal. To Capp and millions of his admirers they are the very essence of interest.

Curiosity, too, is a strong emotional force. Once engendered in the reader it will compel him to find out what happened.

If emotional response is the test of interest, how is it induced? In general terms the components of interest are *organization, tasteful phrasing,* and *color.* Each will be discussed in turn, color in a separate chapter.

(A) *Organization.* Once in a hundred times, a dropped knife will stick in the ground, straight up. This is pure accident. The rest of the time it has to be aimed. Even then failure is far more frequent unless a trained hand guides it.

With equal rarity a reporter encounters a story which practically assembles itself, because all of its essentials are almost equally important *and* absorbing, in whatever order he puts them together. But this too is coincidence.

Story organization is the major element in the process of attracting and holding the reader's attention while we inform him. A certain amount of interest, to be sure, is intrinsic when we do no more than put down active facts in their natural order, as in conversation. A coal miner who experiences a thrilling rescue doesn't have to know how to "write" to gain an audience for his tale. In fact, his unschooled eyewitness account may have an appeal of its own, as evidenced by the effectiveness of verbatim quotes in a professional news story.

Even so, something more is needed to achieve the degree of reader-interest we seek in handling news happenings of varying degree between the lurid and the lackluster. The writer does not satisfy this extra need by accident any oftener than the knife will stick when tossed at random. His is the product of design, a distinct part of his function.

Some disorganized stories switch the reader's attention back and forth confusingly. Others bore him because the writer slavishly adheres too closely to conventional patterns in assembling his account. The latter fault has ruined many a feature story, wherein ingenuity and freshness are far more formidable than formula. In either case the reader's interest is lost—if indeed it is ever gained at all.

Jack Quigg, Associated Press news editor in Los Angeles, expressed it this way in a staff bulletin during one of AP's writing campaigns:

> The stories that draw praise are those that keep the reader reading to the end. Be they fifty word brights or five hundred word "think" pieces, they have what it takes to sustain interest. This quality of hooking the reader and keeping him hooked isn't a natural attribute of news stories. It's one the writer must build in. The talented reporter takes time to devise the best way of organizing the words in a sentence, the sentences in the paragraph, and the paragraphs in an integrated story with impact.

Now comes the obvious inquiry: How do we do this?

Before we even start we must be certain we realize, and remember, that in essence there are only two prime questions involved in arranging story material:

Will the finished piece report the news?

Will it be interesting or emotionally moving?

If the writer can answer both questions affirmatively, he has marshaled his details in successful sequence.

This leaves him a great deal of latitude: it is not solely a matter of following the old Five-W formula. In many instances there are several ways to answer both questions positively.

For example, you have no doubt noticed from time to time that reporters for two opposing papers have approached the same story from different angles, both of which proved to be effective. This is not invariably successful, but it happens. More often, one wire service will take the play away from the other service by emphasizing angles that the other has subordinated or omitted.

This is one of the expectable hazards of newspaper writing. Our chief concern here is the handling of story organization in general terms.

It is a practical fact that most daily occurrences are not equally informative *and* interesting; one or the other quality predominates. Which is strongest in the case at hand? Does the news value require the greater emphasis, or is the human appeal paramount?

Organization really begins at this point. To illustrate, here are the four main situations the reporter is most likely to encounter:

1. *Strong news, strong interest.* Dominating this category are the "big" stories of action and violence—shipwrecks, mysterious slayings of prominent persons, major fires, hurricanes, floods, and other spectacular disasters. Their prime news value is a matter of *loss*—in lives, injuries, money, property. Recalling the analogy of the dropped knife, we could say that newspaper accounts of such occurrences probably come closest to organizing themselves because even the unembellished details of *what happened* carry a high degree of built-in interest. In such cases it is quite possible for the reporter to tell the news and simultaneously to capture the attention of his reader merely by relating the facts. The consequences and the circumstances under which they take place constitute details which are inherently interesting in themselves, and thus do not necessarily require a special format to create or enhance emotional impact.

Although a poor account probably will hold the reader in reporting occurrences of this type, the skilled writer will (a) arrange details in the order of their news and atmospheric value (color); (b) make certain he has omitted none of the essential facts (a failure which invariably raises unanswered questions in the reader's mind).

In doing this, the reporter has supplemented *intrinsic* interest with interest that is *generated* by the sequence in which he tells his story.

Thus the story embodying strong news and strong interest remains the easiest to assemble; the leg work involved is far more difficult than the writing. Fortunately or unfortunately, the "big" stories do not develop every day. Far more frequent are the reporting chores entailed in the remaining categories.

2. *Strong news, weak interest.* When the facts are significant

but emotionally inactive, listing details in the order of their news importance and atmospheric value will produce, too often, a routine and dull account. Here interest must be *induced.* This requires an arrangement of detail which will inspire a reader response. His attention must be attracted and held while we feed him information that is important but not in itself appealing. Facts, quotes, and other story angles are arranged according to their interest value first, their news importance second. This, to be sure, is contrary to the normal treatment of strong news and for a very good reason: communication has failed if we lose the reader in the process of informing him, no matter how vital the information may be.

Our problem here is exemplified by complex subject matter and/or highly involved circumstances. Technical reports provide common examples. In dealing with them it may be necessary to offer lesser facts first, to grab the reader, or to change in some other way the normal who-what-why-when-where sequences of news-worthy but tedious facts. Stories about legal, fiscal, and governmental affairs or scientific achievements are characteristic.

The writer's best advice for creating reader interest in dry facts is the technique of making his audience feel personally related to these heavier types of subject matter. A good tax story, for instance, cannot consist of statistics alone. It must show the reader-listener, by analogy or by other basic terms he can readily understand, exactly how a higher or lower levy will affect his purse. If he is given a picture of the advantages to his own family of, let us say, a new park and at the same time apprised of the economic sacrifice he and his neighbors will have to make to acquire it, he is far more likely to *react*—favorably or unfavorably. In either case his interest has been sparked.

The aforementioned Dr. Flesch strongly recommends this use of the human, or personal, element when interest must be gathered by the writer. The reporter causes the reader to relate, in some way, to whatever is said or done. Flesch uses as an example a complicated medical story which could easily be a boring, semi-intelligible account because the average reader has little knowledge in the field.

He starts with a specific case history, real or hypothetical. Here is the experience of John Doe, who could be any of the story's readers. Doe develops unusual symptoms. They persist despite conventional therapy. Alarmed, he consults specialists, who make a diagnosis. They are familiar with research in the area of Doe's illness, and Doe enters a university hospital where this investigation is being conducted. He submits to new techniques, and his reactions are recounted.

All of this is presented quickly and, above all, simply; it must neither consume too many words nor veer into technical discussion.

The reader, lured by narrative, feels himself relating to another real person. He now "takes his medicine" willingly: he is ready for the solid scientific information the reporter seeks to transmit.

This is an instance in which briefly delaying the hard news is justified because interest has been created. Had the reporter followed the conventional procedure of offering first the scientific discovery—as in the average spot news story—very likely he would have lost most of his readers at once by stuffing them with confusing technical facts in the first few paragraphs.

Other forms of illustration can be substituted for the case history. Example: reconstruction of a dramatic scene in the laboratory when a scientific breakthrough takes place. In this approach John Doe's experience might not be included at all, or it might occupy the last part of the story instead of the first.

Many times a conversational approach is an effective way to grab and hold the reader prior to delivering a complicated message. A wire service correspondent employed this method successfully in starting his story with a courtroom question-and-answer sequence. This ran a hundred and fifty words before the legal technicalities involved were presented, but the story was widely used across the country by editors who knew their audiences would be intrigued by its unconventional design.

3. *Weak news, strong interest.*   Here we encounter the typical feature story. The subject matter may be infinitely diverse—animate or inanimate—and the structure equally varied—from the conventional to the bizarre. Anniversaries, personal achievements, historical landmarks, unusual ways of living or working, artistic collections, hobbies are merely a few of its topics in an almost endless list. Similarly, the story form lends itself to all manner of techniques, including chronological narrative, the tale that tells itself in quotes, the suspense account with its "kicker," or tag line, at the end. In other forms the writer poses a catchy question, then lines up details as steps leading to the answer, or he may start his account with a relatively unimportant situation which creates atmosphere receptive to reader interest.

The news is not forgotten. But, because the primary purpose of such accounts is to *stimulate,* informative matter is woven into the mass of interest-producing details. The news, being weak, is not emphasized, Generally speaking, the personal element is paramount; we are telling the traditional "human interest" story, in one guise or another. The reporter selects the angle and pattern he regards as most likely to appeal to the greatest number of readers.

Garden-variety anniversary features are well known to us all: the professional athlete, for instance, who lost a leg in the South Pacific and in the ensuing twenty-five years made himself an outstanding insurance agent by means of a telephone and an imaginative sales pitch.

Another, rather more novel, example of an interesting feature was the story written by a wire service correspondent[*] whose idea sprang from the old carol "The Twelve Days of Christmas," in which "my true love" bestows, on each of the twelve days, such gifts as a partridge in a pear tree, collie birds, swimming swans, milking maids, French hens and so forth, up to and including "twelve lords a-leaping." The reporter's story offered these as suggestions "for the man who has everything," delineating how and at what cost each item in the list might be procured by a whimsi-

[*] David Smith, Los Angeles Associated Press Bureau, Christmas, 1964.

cal gift-giver with more money than good sense. The result was a humorous and highly successful holiday feature.

Outstanding members of this third category are the interpretive "think" piece, the profile, and the backgrounder. All are enjoying greater space in newspapers and more time on the air than ever before. "Reporting in depth" has become a Space Age cliché, in reference to the interpretive story that pursues "the news behind the news" by "digging" for additional aspects beyond the obvious. Widely practiced by wire services, networks, and the more progressive individual newspapers, this analytical approach has been an important factor in the contemporary effort to improve the image and prestige of news media. The backgrounder, similarly, has become a necessary adjunct to reporting in a world where speed is a dominant force. Prior to the astonishing growth of electronic facilities for communication, even small dailies filled a few pages with difficulty; now the problem is reversed. There is, for example, no room to bring the reader up to date each day in the progress of a bill through congressional channels. When an important piece of legislation reaches a critical or otherwise significant stage, the background story serves a needful purpose in reviewing what has transpired during weeks of committee hearings and has, perhaps, been forgotten by the average reader-listener. In the same way, when revolution or some catastrophic act of God ravages a remote and little-known country, the backgrounder gives meaning to the hard news of the event itself.

Quite frequently the same function is performed by the profile, when the occurrence involves a personality. The following leads, quoted from Associated Press profiles, will indicate how this variety of feature can be used to whet interest:

> The new president of the American Federation of Musicians hasn't played the violin in twenty years.

> Gen. Jacques-Emile Massu, who heads a defiant emergency regime in Algeria, is a man in a hurry with fiery eyes and a bearlike manner.

"I was born in the wrong century," Zsa Zsa Gabor once told me. "I would have made a bum out of Madame Pompadour."

Interpretives, backgrounds, and profiles customarily are presented as sidebars to straight news accounts and therefore are concerned primarily with interest even though they are pegged to the news and are, in a secondary sense, informative.

4. *Weak news, weak interest.* Most often this is the "cute" story of little or no consequence that nonetheless appeals to the reader purely by means of the writer's cleverness in designing its structure. It is almost always brief, and the sky is the only limit to the manner he chooses in achieving readability. It may have only a single interesting detail and no news value whatever. Boxes and "brites" are examples in this field, where the gimmicky approach prevails. Because it lacks any semblance of importance, or at best boasts very little, it can even be written end-first-beginning-last, if this fits the reporter's fancy without distorting the truth. A routine robbery in which the criminal is slain thus becomes a "must read" item under the treatment this Miami wire service man gave it, in seventy-five words:

> "Don't say anything," Patrolman Ralph Rex cautioned his companion at a crowded restaurant. "I'll wait until he gets his hands on the trays."
>
> Customers sat frozen in their chairs last night as a masked gunman scooped up cash register trays containing $800 and shouldered through the doors. Rex fired three shots into his back. The bandit fell dead.
>
> Police Chief Karl Engle promoted Rex on the spot to sergeant. The bandit was not identified immediately.

What news the piece has is subordinated to technique.

The reverse process is used again in this narrative report of not very much at all:

> LAKEWOOD, N.J. (AP)—Once upon a time—in fact, it seems like yesterday—a little girl took a trip to Grandma's house.
>
> When she got there, the little girl left her parents and started

playing with two little friends. Pretty soon they found themselves a half mile from the house. They decided to go back, and her friends took the long way around.

But the little girl, let's call her Joyce Gunther, 8, of Howell Township, decided to take a shortcut through the dense scrub pine forest.

Joyce didn't meet a wolf. In fact, she didn't meet anybody, and it wasn't long before she realized she was lost and started getting frightened.

Her parents got frightened too, and they called some volunteer woodsmen—250 of them.

And since this is a modern fairy tale, a helicopter from the Lakehurst Naval Air Station also joined in the search over the four-square-mile wooded tract.

A group of volunteer firemen finally came on the little girl. She had been lost for twelve hours but she was safe and sound.

The woodsmen went home and the helicopter went back to its hangar.

Stories written in this manner are almost impossible to cut without destruction of their appeal, and the two cited above were properly brief—one less than a hundred words, the other fewer than two hundred.

The *unusual* treatment can be applied, in a certain degree, to many stories in all categories. The first—strong news, strong interest—would be the most likely exception, and even in that classification unconventional organization frequently is effective. Most reporters attempt it too seldom; the average issue of a newspaper contains too few stories that generate interest through offbeat handling.

During the second AP Writing Campaign a few years ago the directing committee took this stand: the majority of working wire service reporters quickly spot the essentials of a story and plow right in. Usually they do a solid job, but not always an imaginative job. The latter requires *special thinking before* writing, so that, without abrogating his objective point of view, the writer produces the most appealing account. The AP found that a "much higher percentage of bellringers" issued from those reporters who took the committee's advice.

It is good for the writer and good for the reader to get out of the rut now and then. Of course, bizarre techniques should not be overemphasized lest they belittle, hint at contempt or otherwise violate good taste, and stories employing them certainly cannot comprise too much of a newspaper's content because they can't be shortened easily.

Jack Quigg, quoted earlier in this chapter, advises:

"When you start to write, give consideration to an unconventional approach. You can always come back to the routine style, which may be the most effective after all." *

Whatever the ratio of news and interest may be, the appropriate organization of every story should be anticipated. Some false starts and a certain amount of rewriting are inevitable. But, just as he should learn to rough out his lead in his head on his way to the telephone or back to his office, the competent reporter should develop the ability to produce a mental blueprint of his story's plan before he dictates or writes the first word.

This takes thought and practice. It is not a process obtainable wholly from a book, in the manner of memorizing rules or multiplication tables. Of some help, however, will be the study of stories reflecting faulty organization.

Here is a typical example: a sports reporter covering a horse race phrased a very readable lead pegged to the breaking of a local track record. But thereafter he (1) waited five paragraphs to state which record was broken; (2) buried deep in his account the weights carried, a significant detail in this race; (3) neglected to explain, until the very last sentence, a dramatic switch of jockeys; (4) omitted entirely the fact that the victorious horse failed by a very narrow margin to become the world's leading money winner. All of these facts should have appeared high in the story. A classic error in building the straight news account is the failure to recog-

* AP Writing Campaign bulletin, "Organizing a Story," June 16, 1958.

nize the most important elements and relate them as quickly as possible without cluttering sentences or paragraphs.

In another case, a story about three persons dead and two missing in an earthquake delayed until the sixth paragraph the dramatic fact that the temblor lifted the end of an island twenty feet and dumped it into the sea. This belonged higher in the story for reasons of both news and color: two of the known victims were lost there.

High in the story also is the place for conditional details, if any. These are facts subject to change, such as this one: "Additional statements by Starkweather are expected to be filed with the court later in the day." But perhaps they won't be. If absolutely necessary, such material should occupy a separate paragraph near the lead, where it can be easily and briefly "subbed" or "topped" with a new lead, as developments require. In the case cited, the additional statements were filed, shortly after the noon recess. But the paragraph containing the above sentence and other conditional matter appeared so far down in the original account that twelve-thirteenths of the story had to be rewritten for the home edition.

Organization stands very close to the editing process. The story with the best structural design is the easiest to update, amplify, or alter otherwise. This is vital in stories of the first category—strong news, strong interest—which may run for days, changing from hour to hour. Under these circumstances it is usually wisest to ignore, in the day's original account, the conditional matter that is non-essential. Then, when the development takes place, the fresh material can be inserted or made part of a concise new lead, depending upon its news import.

There is, too, a way of phrasing interest-bearing but conditional detail so that it will "stand up" in spite of developments. The reporter is asking for trouble if he writes: "Chief Jones says the fire will be near control by sundown if favorable wind conditions prevail." This is a "mousetrap." Like as not, rising gusts will fan the flames to fury again in midafternoon. But an equally inconclusive statement can be presented safely by phrasing it in the past tense:

"Early in the afternoon Chief Jones said he believed the fire could be controlled by sundown, barring a change in the wind." Whatever happens, such a sentence could remain in the original story. If several paragraphs consist of conditional matter, such a trick will save a considerable portion of the original story.

Sometimes organization and editing clash through no fault of the writer's original plan. Take, for instance, a well-knit story presenting the dramatic details of a double shooting. Later in the day it became necessary to cover the activities of a posse and other developments that followed the crime. These required two hundred words in a new lead which buried the drama and thus damaged the story's color value. Although this happens to be a wire service example, the same situation is common enough in writing for individual newspapers. The wire service, to save transmission time, merely topped the story with developments. Properly, the new lead should have incorporated some of the dramatic details, picking up lower in the original account. This would have required three hundred or three hundred fifty words for the new top, instead of two hundred, with commensurate loss of wire time. But the resulting appeal of the story would have been worth it.

Similarly many newspapers economize on typesetting, yet the best publications will sacrifice time, space, and metal to put the good story in sharp focus—its informational and emotional portions in proper emphasis—so that the printed product is an *organized* entity.

Damon Runyon, in his column *The Brighter Side,* said in 1945: "The artistic phase of reporting is the ability to put not only fact into the story but color and human interest, also feeling and good taste. The last elements are, I think, the most important."

(B) *Taste and tone.* Judicious *choice of detail is* a distinctive factor in producing the taste and emotional appeal Runyon preferred.

The details we select, and the way we present them, must be appropriate to the nature of the event. It would, for instance, be difficult to imagine any reporter writing such a sentence as: "His grandmother was chopped up by a streetcar." Yet ill-advised and often flippant presentations of the facts characterize the style in which many overly eager young writers strive to grab reader interest. Their result is just the opposite. By their poor judgment such writers repel rather than attract.

Writing isn't words alone. Through suitability and discernment the reporter must also establish the mood, or tone, of the event. A typical, if not spectacular, example is this sentence:

> Argentine President Frondizi tonight emerged *shaken but at least temporarily safe from a rebellious challenge to the nation's armed forces.*

Enemies of taste and tone—and thus potential destroyers of interest—are stories reflecting such faults as *imprecision, pretentious phrasing, and superfluous quotations.* Imprecision is the product of generalization; that is, nonspecific detail and broad, inconclusive statements. The following imprecise sentence says next to nothing but the obvious:

> Assuming nothing drastic occurs in the foreseeable future, what will happen in 1997 when the British lease on the new territories (exclusive of tiny Hong Kong Island) runs out seems to be anyone's grim guess.

Such pointless observations turn up far too frequently in foreign correspondence. The writer really has nothing *specific* to report. In this instance no one can forecast precisely events decades hence, although everybody can guess. Merely saying so embodies no reader interest whatever.

Imprecision in another form results when the writer fails to support such adjectives as "funny," "dramatic," or "exciting" without specific evidence. The lead of a wire service story read: "Casey Stengel, in his own *unfathomable* way, told senators today . . ." Nothing "unfathomable" followed.

Descriptive nouns standing all alone produce the same unsatisfactory effect upon readers. The same story, in a later paragraph, contained this sentence: "Stengel kept the senators and the audience in *guffaws.*" Nothing funny followed.

The tone of the story and the reader's interest demand answers to the questions raised by "unfathomable" and "guffaws."

Furthermore, both story mood and subsequent reader appeal would be strengthened if the *precise details* alone had been cited. The reader then would have reached his own conclusion as to what was unfathomable or funny.

Nonspecific sentences frequently are newsless, and therefore dull:

> The United Auto Workers Union today virtually completed tabulation of strike authorization votes at three big plants.

The specific fact, contained in a later paragraph, was that even the incomplete tally overwhelmingly favored a walkout. This should have been the lead.

It would be foolish to assume, of course, that *all* precise details enhance mood and inspire interest. The following sentence is specific but it has little appeal for the daily newspaper reader; it might attract the attention of a special audience if it appeared in a trade journal:

> Thirty-two U.S. supplemental and large irregular air carriers were named winners today of the National Safety Council's aviation safety award for 1957.

Pretentious writing distorts the established tone of a story and sometimes even creates a new mood not in keeping with the atmosphere of the event. Here is an example of an overblown figure of speech which violates taste:

> The 1938 earthquake sloshed Lituya Bay *like a palsied person passing the gravy boat.*

Such a simile may be descriptive, but it is also flippant and inimical to the nature of the event being reported. What's amusing about an earthquake? And what's cute about palsy? The very best phraseology will jar the reader if it is inappropriate for the subject at hand or out of place in the development of the story.

Here is an example of phrasing which suits neither the man nor the occurrence:

> Lt. Gov. Frazar tonight rammed his hand into the crumbling dike of Louisiana government.

There is nothing wrong with the sentence grammatically. To be sure, the metaphor is trite. But the true fault here is that, to readers even moderately informed, the sentence borders on the ridiculous because for days news accounts had emphasized Frazar's supercaution, portraying him as a man of indecision. The statement might be apt in reference to the late Gov. Long, but applied to Frazar it is out of character and unconvincing almost to the point of being unbelievable.

The pretentious writer often becomes so enamored of his own words that he forgets the news. Not until the last two words do we get an inkling of what the following sentence is all about:

> The banshee howls of mighty engines will dash their echoes against the peopled cliffs here Sunday when America's 1958 thunderboat season opens with the second annual running of the Apple Cup *speedboat race.*

Pompous phrasing wastes words and encourages confusion:

> Insofar as his possible resignation is concerned, however, they did not foreclose the possibility that it might be forthcoming in the near future.

This is merely the fat way of saying "they didn't deny he might quit soon." Such verbosity may be a hangover from the generation when reporters were paid by the word. Again it becomes obvious that the simplified sentence is the best safeguard against the trap of ponderous writing because it is clear, specific, and thrifty. Another example:

> Biochemists engaged in brain research have come upon significant relationships between body chemistry and mental disorders, a group of doctors said today.

Straightforwardly stated, this means:

Scientists have linked mental ailments to changes in body chemistry.

Complex and portentous constructions usually are dull:

Sen. Wayne Morse announced today he has requested hearings by the Senate Agriculture Committee on a House-passed bill to change the present formula under which 25 per cent of gross receipts from national forests are paid to counties in lieu of taxes.

Divested of its excess baggage, this sentence would read:

Sen. Wayne Morse said today he has asked for hearings on a House-passed bill changing the basis of allocating national forest revenue to counties.

Two sentences would follow:

At present counties get 25 per cent of gross receipts, instead of taxes.
The Senate Agriculture Committee would conduct the hearings.

Ostentatious writing always sounds self-conscious, affected. Let us close this section with one more illustration, which will need no comment. It is the complete sentence from which examples of gobbledegook were cited in chapter III (p. 38).*

The sustention of this principle is all the more important where, as here, the forces at work to frustrate the constitution and the authority of the federal courts were deliberately set in motion by the government of the state whose school system is under mandate to achieve conformity with the constitution.

Unnecessary quotations exercise a remarkably bad effect upon the taste and tone of a story. The dedicated search for direct quotations, usually regarded as a high virtue in news writing, can be carried to absurd lengths. These, in marring the mood of the re-

*This, happily, is not a newspaper sentence at all, but an excerpt from a judicial ruling.

porter's account, reduce the reader's interest and delay him as well.

For instance, unless the interviewer is trying to demonstrate that his subject is a dull fellow indeed, no value at all will be added to the story by such a quote as this:

"There are Japanese and there are Japanese," the prince said. "Some do and some do not have hard feelings."

Omitting the obvious fact often strengthens the atmosphere of a story. This is well illustrated by a partial-quote sentence included in a story about prisoners who were trapped in a roaring fire set by an insane convict. Six well-written paragraphs contained wisely chosen details to convey dramatically the horror of their experience. Then, anticlimactically, came a needless understatement, fracturing the mood that the writer had established so painstakingly:

Levon said the death screams "were frightening."

An otherwise well-handled story was flawed by this inane quote-for-the-sake-of-quotation:

Despite the umbrella, the President was quite wet by the time he made it to the car. But he was cheerful, remarking with a grin: "It looks like you're having a little rain here."

Had it been uttered by anyone other than a chief of state, such an observation would never have been quoted.

Partial quotes, silly or not, are highly overworked in newspaper copy. Theodore M. Bernstein, Assistant Managing Editor of *The New York Times,* said in one of his staff bulletins:

"There is no need to quote words which have no particular significance simply because they are taken from quoted statements. Why say, for instance, that Igor Cassini was alleged to have written Trujillo to 'assure' him of the 'help' of the Hearst newspapers? . . . If a word is used with a special meaning or if the context gives it abnormal significance, by all means quote it. But otherwise the quotes may puzzle the reader or induce him to read some unintended importance into a word that is just minding its own business." *

Attitude

The foregoing discussion of STYLE and INTEREST brings us to the third area of news writing in which a need for improvement is strongly indicated: the *attitude* of the writer.

In 1958 the Associated Press undertook to survey its entire news report for flaws and fine points, a monumental project that occupied a committee full-time for nearly two years. Informally, the review is still going on. The committee gave its program this premise:

"It is our experience that abstract essays on how to produce better prose are less effective than frank discussion of writers' faults, with emphasis on specific examples."

Within a matter of months the committee was able to report marked progress. Leads were shorter, punchier. Story length had been reduced. And—the point which is pertinent here—there was far more bright, offbeat writing. Staffers were thinking more sharply, yet they had relaxed. They were breaking away from the routine, trying new approaches when their mood, and the material, permitted.

Some of these attempts were not successful, of course, but the over-all result was well worth the effort.

(A) *Think!* Perhaps the most important conclusion produced by the survey was this: among journeyman reporters, ignorance had very little to do with error. Carelessness was the culprit. And, as the program progressed, it became apparent that most of the drab, stilted writing was due to the failure to *think.* It followed

*From *Winners & Sinners,* December 13, 1963.

that *haste* was responsible, more often than not, for the writers' failure to think.

The AP Writing Committee was dealing with professional reporters and editors, to be sure, but the survey's premise holds equally true for students of the craft.

In an earlier chapter, concerned with word choice for the good and simple sentence, it was pointed out that grammatical accuracy does not insure reader comprehension. A perfectly correct sentence sometimes fails to reflect the meaning it was intended to convey. Writer and reader, in such a case, have not really communicated; the message has gone astray. The writer has not said what he meant to say.

Numerous examples of this fault were cited in the survey, and here is a very obvious addition:

> The champagne flowed like wine.

The reporter knew better, yet he produced a redundancy—and it eluded editors.

What happened? Why did he make such an obvious mistake? The answer is very simple: he didn't think. He lapsed momentarily from the state of awareness that the journalist's obligation at all times is to say what he means and mean what he says. Failure to think is just as evident in story content as it is in syntax.

Confronted with their mistakes, errant writers usually will confess that they "knew better."

The champagne error doesn't mislead anyone, but the fact remains that an awkward statement can be dangerous if it concerns a serious situation. Most often it transmits only part of the writer's message. Sometimes, however, it actually says the exact opposite of what he had in mind, as in this instance:

> A forty-four-year-old newspaper publisher *who never has held public office* was selected by Republicans today to *regain* the governor's office.

What the writer meant has only been indicated, not said. The publisher cannot *regain* what he has never had. The undelivered message here was:

> *Republicans,* campaigning to *regain* the governorship, have chosen as their candidate a forty-four-year-old publisher who has never held public office.

Think *before* you write—think *while* you write—never write faster than you think, whatever the deadline may be.

Choosing the correct word is basic in saying what we mean. And only failure to think prevented the proper selection by the reporter who wrote this:

> Hogue is in excellent health except for a hearing defect. A widower, he is *survived* by six children.

Again, the reporter did not say what he meant to say when he misplaced the parenthetical phrase "while cycling" in the following:

> Nine-year-old Belinda Eltzoth was *kidnaped, raped,* and *strangled while cycling* to the grocery store last night.

The action thus suggested is patently impossible. Had he thought for a moment, the writer would have told us that Belinda was on her way to the grocery store by bicycle when she was kidnaped, raped, then strangled.

Two sentences would have been chosen if the writer had stopped to think before rushing to tell everything at once in this distracting statement:

> The beaten body of twenty-three-year-old Anne Kaufman, *who resumed her maiden name after her divorce* was washed ashore in Boston September 19, the day after the freighter *Utrecht* left for Brooklyn.

Omission of the comma after "divorce" made the sentence even worse.

(B) *Inertia.* The habit of thinking constantly about what he is going to say next is an essential attitude of every competent writer. If he doesn't, he'll make a mistake. Furthermore, after a certain period of time and a certain number of such errors, he will attain the state of mental inertia, wherein the habit he has formed is the *failure* to think.

Naturally, the situation is complicated when it includes a faulty concept of grammar. In this connection our earlier discussion of the dangling modifier may be recalled with profit:

> In ill health in recent years, Guest's syndicated daily poem appeared in nearly three hundred newspapers at the height of his popularity.

A famous product of inertia is the humdrum view of all occurrences. There is, after all, a pattern to the daily flow of routine news, and the reporter very quickly becomes familiar with it. After a few years he will tend to feel that he has written every story at least once before—or one very much like it. This tendency must be resisted; unless he is careful he will find boredom creeping up on him. He may take a cynical attitude toward certain types of news stories; for days on end he may find nothing really "new" in the world.

Once established, inertia impedes the urge to devise brighter, more appealing story treatment. The easiest—and least effective —way to write about a romantic triangle is the way you wrote about the last one, or the last twenty-five. A vast number of similar situations recur in news happenings. These, perhaps more than the unique event, need special treatment to attract the reader. Special treatment is based on extra thought.

This is the point at which the reporter must renew his enthusiasm. When everything seems to have achieved the status of a cliché he must break out of the "vicious circle" and shun the "beaten path." Let him take a flier, report his conventional situation in an unconventional way. The story may wind up in the wastebasket, but if it does come off it probably will be a bell-ringer.

Enterprise is inertia's opposite. We can hunt for the unusual twist that lifts the story above the level of the ordinary. We can dig for the less obvious facts, make one more phone call in search of a telling quote. We can build up a routine pronouncement by expanding secondary angles. In all likelihood the result will be worthy of the extra questions, the deeper research.

Earlier in this chapter it was stated that the reporter is obligated to interest his readers as well as to inform them. It follows that the reporter is obligated to nurture his own zeal.

If constraint and conformity bore the reader, they also weary the writer and reduce his efficiency. A reader won't find much interest in a piece produced by a writer who can't work up much steam about it himself. But the writer has this advantage over the reader: even when the news is dull he can get interested in the WAY he presents it. He is free to experiment, within reason. He can duck the obvious lead. Sometimes he can report the action in reverse sequence, as we have noticed in the discussion of story organization. To be sure, he has to supply all the essential information, but he doesn't have to deliver it by a route that was old in Caesar's day.

(C) *Relax.* Mental inertia—the extension of failure to think—is not associated solely with boredom and a cynical attitude. Quite often it is a consequence of tension. Easy-to-read, flowing stories very rarely are written by time-harried reporters whose nerves are on edge and whose wits are commensurately dull.

It is true enough that the newspaper business is dominated by the clock. However, a great deal of harm has been done—to budding young reporters and to the quality of newspapers as well—by overemphasis on the speed factor.

City editors probably are chiefly responsible. By tradition they are always in a hurry. Unfortunately, there is often no better reason than tradition. As every veteran knows, editors have developed over the years far more than their fair share of shibboleths and superstitions. These can confound the beginner and even have been known to ruin him completely as a reporter. The city editor who will wait as long as he possibly can before heckling the new writer is wise indeed, and rare.

Those city desk men who yell continually about the deadline will maintain that they got that way because they had to put up with a staff overloaded with dopes who couldn't write their own names in less than five minutes. But in the majority of cases their argument is specious.

Deadlines are important, and so is enough speed to meet them. But many potentially fine writers react contrarily to the cattle-prod technique. And the same editors who use it would be the first to admit that thought produces a better story than haste.

What they really want, of course, is both. But most are unwilling to wait for experience to generate such speed and skill.

Faced with such a double order, the neophyte reporter may freeze up entirely, defeating his own and his editor's primary purpose. His best recourse is to concentrate on *relaxing*. He will think better and faster.

A simple, relaxed approach to news writing pays off in many ways. The product is easier to read because it sounds as if it were easier to write. And it is actually easier to write once we have learned to relax. There is no really good reason why tension should be an integral part of the process. Naturally, there will be occasions when tension is inescapable, and a certain amount sharpens the style of some writers. This, however, is a state of *controlled enthusiasm*, not a fear of failure. It is engendered by a particularly dramatic occurrence, not by the bulk of the daily news output.

Another dividend of the relaxed writing habit is fewer errors. Many an enlightened city editor has proved this. The AP survey also showed that reporters who let themselves go just a bit made far fewer mistakes than did the writers who sweated, worried about the rules, and, ultimately, froze to their typewriters, unable to start a sentence.

To encourage this atmosphere of relaxation a few perceptive editors have urged their staff people to adopt a conversational style as often as the subject matter permits. Write as if you were telling your mother, at the dinner table, what you saw or heard this afternoon. Every good city editor knows the efficacy of this. When a reporter phones his office to outline what he has, his description very often is much clearer, much more concise, and far more dramatic than the story he ultimately puts on paper—purely because he is *talking* instead of *writing*.

It goes without saying that the chatty approach should not be too colloquial.

Writing is hard work. But it can be fun, too, if we relax. It is quite possible to become a Liberace of the typewriter keyboard.

V

Descriptive Writing— The Quest for Color

The Initial Approach: Facts vs. Adjectives

Color in writing has certain abstract qualities, about which it is pointless to generalize. All of us envy those imaginative and facile phrasemakers who have an innate gift for brilliant description, a natural ability to find humor in the commonplace or crystal clarity in the complex.

But such writers are unique; they probably will develop with or without formal guidance. For the vast remainder of us, there are certain techniques which can produce color to one degree or another in descriptive writing, and these are highly useful to the newsman who must write rapidly.

The emotional potency of facts. The sensitive and observant reporter will realize very early in his career that *facts alone* are capable of generating color in the great majority of situations he will encounter. This is true because facts can and do create emotional reactions. They are, to put it another way, *affective*.

This primary discovery by the new reporter is followed almost at once by the realization that the emotional power of facts usually is far greater than the decorative value of adjectives, which—too often—are mere abstractions, basically unrealistic and therefore almost meaningless in the process of *informing* the reader-listener.

"The greatest parade in Rossville's history" conveys nothing to the person who has never seen Rossville and even little enough to the people who live there. But "ten thousand horses, sixteen brass bands, and forty thousand marching school children" are facts which provide at least some degree of color in portraying an impressive event for residents and strangers alike. They establish an environment which is completely lacking in the adjectival description of a parade as the "greatest" in history.

The semanticist S. I. Hayakawa has recorded a number of situations illustrating the use of facts alone to generate high emotional impact. Such occurrences, usually somewhat extreme, can be documented coldly and without any embellishment whatever. Here is one example he cites:

> Although no anesthetics or surgical instruments were available, he said the leg would have to be amputated. He performed the operation, therefore, with a butcher knife and a hatchet, while four men held the patient down.

Adjectives, whatever their number or degree, could not possibly have heightened the horror which the writer achieved with facts alone. In commenting upon his example, Hayakawa says:

"Instead of telling the reader 'it was a ghastly operation!' we can make the reader say it for himself. The reader is, so to speak, made to participate by being forced to draw his own conclusions."

It is, of course, this sense of realism that hits the reader-listener squarely between the eyes. Facts are the essence of realism. Most adjectives are abstractions. The means and manner of a "brutal" murder are more graphic than the word quoted in this sentence. Such catch-all phrases as "*bitter* custody battle," "*vicious* tornado," and *"ugly-tempered* mob" save a certain number of words, and that is probably why they turn up with such distressing frequency in newspaper copy. But for journalistic purposes they save words in the wrong way. They leave the reader suspended because they are not specific; they present only a shadowy outline of the word picture, whereas facts will fill it in. The adjective is quicker than the detail, but weaker, too. The reader much prefers to be told, in reasonable length, *what* the recriminatory testimony was in the custody fight, *what* the tornado damaged, *how* the mob showed its temper.

Small details. The importance of the facts themselves is not necessarily an element in engendering this kind of color. More often than not, the minor details are the most potent in helping the writer to set the scene or to heighten the atmosphere in which the action takes place. Although they may not have anything directly to do with the occurrence itself, they are highly important in establishing the emotional background, for which *mood* is another term.

Facial and auditory descriptions, presented factually, are commonplace examples of this technique: the twitch above the lawyer's right eye, the ambassador's manner of greeting other distinguished persons, the scientist's preoccupation with his pencil or his eyeglasses.

Sound images can be particularly impressive. In a story describing the summing-up speech of Clarence Darrow, the writer pointed out that the famous lawyer timed his climax with the tolling of 12 o'clock by the courthouse bells. Darrow synchronized each main point with each stroke of the hour.

The experienced journalist looks long and hard for details that enable the reader to "see" an event. When he watches a senator—angered in debate—pound a table with his fist, the veteran writer does not merely report, "The senator became angry." Instead, he describes the scene as did one reporter who observed Joseph McCarthy: "Senator McCarthy banged his fist on the table and the glasses jumped."

Antoine de Saint-Exupéry once discussed Joseph Conrad's meticulous attention to detail as follows:

> When Conrad described a typhoon he said very little about towering waves, or darkness, or the whistling of the wind in the shrouds. He knew better. Instead, he took the reader down into the hold of the vessel, packed with emigrant coolies, where the rolling and the pitching of the ship had ripped up and scattered their bags and bundles, burst open their boxes and flung their humble belongings into a crazy heap.
>
> Family treasures painfully collected in a lifetime of poverty, pitiful mementos so alike that nobody but their owners could have told them apart, had lost their identity and lapsed into chaos, into anonymity, into an amorphous magma.

David Lancashire of the Associated Press used the same technique when he depicted the aftermath of an earthquake in Iran by telling about a child's bewilderment:

> The little boy's face was stained with dried blood. He knelt beside the neatly wrapped bodies of his mother, father, and seven brothers and sisters. Banging his head in the dust, he cried, "What shall I do, God, what shall I do?"

Frequently the details can be presented in narrative form. In 1952 President-elect Eisenhower was accompanied to Korea by Charles E. Wilson, head of the General Motors Corp. and Eisenhower's choice for Secretary of Defense Here's an excerpt from Don Whitehead's AP story about the trip:

> After breakfast, the General agreed to go back up to Suribachi so that cameramen could get the picture they had missed the day before. He rode in a Chevrolet sedan to the foot of Suribachi and then climbed out to transfer to a jeep for the steep climb up a dusty trail cut out of the side of the hill.
>
> Wilson asked the driver why the change was being made from the sedan to the jeep.
>
> "That hill's too steep for the Chevrolet to make it," the driver said.
>
> "Are you sure?" Wilson asked.
>
> "I'm damned sure, sir," the youth replied.

In 1961 an airliner crash in Illinois killed seventy-eight persons, including four twenty-year-old women from Suncook, New Hampshire. Far down in the UPI story was the glimpse of the tragedy:

> In Suncook, a town of three thousand, the chairman of the board of selectmen, clenched a pipe stem in his teeth and fought back tears.
> "I knew them well," he said. "They were good girls. Every one of them."

A Reuters dispatch, telling about a plane crash that wiped out one fifth of the population of the Swiss village Humlikon, used this quote:

> "I wish I had been on the plane," one old man told newsmen. "All the young adults are dead and who is going to do the farming?"

Sometimes detail can be merged with humor, adding to the impact of the phrase or story. When Antony Armstrong-Jones became a member of Britain's House of Lords, UPI said:

> With this quaint ceremony completed, Tony acquires a number of privileges—including the right to be hanged with a silken cord rather than common hemp.

The "cool courage" of John Glenn, America's first man in orbit, was aptly described by newsmen. But they also said he was a "balding, red-haired Marine."

Crime stories, of course, offer a wealth of revealing facts. When a school principal in Indianapolis killed two teachers while several pupils watched, the AP's wrapup night lead included these brief but illuminating phrases: the fifth-graders' "giggles that turned to screams"; the principal killed himself in the woods "where he often hunted"; he "neatly tidied up his desk" before the shootings; three cigarette butts around the body showed "he had sat in thought before killing himself."

Life magazine relied on detail for color in telling how a famous tennis player made his entrance:

When the loudspeaker announces "The Two-Fisted Killer from Ecuador," he rises on short, crooked legs, lowers his shaggy black head, aims himself, and charges onto the court. One arm has a death grip on six tennis rackets. The other, flailing as if to supply additional propulsion, beats the air in a mad circle. With every pigeon-toed stride, his right foot threatens to collide with his left, and he seems certain to disintegrate in a horrible tangle of arms, legs, and rackets. But, with a monstrous sigh, he comes abruptly to rest, determined in spite of his preposterous appearance to play professional tennis. Pancho Segura is onstage.

Theodore M. Bernstein, in his book *Watch Your Language,* offers these examples of detail from *The New York Times:*

"As he talked, Mr. Ben-Gurion was transformed from a rather tired man, suffering from influenza, sitting in a blue bathrobe in a hotel room, to one of his nation's visionaries."

"Few of the 2,000 industrialists who had heard the address were still in the ballroom when Mr. Meany, his teeth clenching a cigar, and Mr. Sligh, a tall, lean furniture manufacturer, confronted each other. The room was loud with the bustle of waiters. . . ."

"Nervously, Maza twisted a yellow pencil in his hands. Dag Hammarskjöld . . . sat impassive at his right, his chin propped on his hand."

Examples of effective use of detail can, of course, be found in books as well as newspapers. Murray Morgan, a former reporter, told in *The Dam* about a visit of Army officers to Grand Coulee. He said:

The young men nodded, and the generals and colonels sucked in their cheeks and looked wise, and then they all got into the staff cars and bounced away over the rutted road.

Obtaining detail—firsthand knowledge of the event. With due respect to rewrite men, the reporter who actually witnesses an event can communicate more effectively what he hears, sees, smells, and feels. He has the facts; the rewrite man, confined to the office, very often must resort to abstract adjectives and other generalizations.

Paul Gallico, a sports writer who became a novelist, based

many of his early feature stories on firsthand information. In 1922 he boxed a round with Jack Dempsey. He caught Dizzy Dean's fast ball in a glove padded with sponge. And he played golf with Bobby Jones and tennis with Vinnie Richards.

Meyer Berger once sat for an hour on a ledge atop a skyscraper, trying to duplicate the thoughts of a woman who had jumped after sitting there for a similar period.

As UPI says: "To get the visceral feel of an event a reporter must be steeped in local color and stand close to the event itself." *

Adjectives can be dangerous. Aside from lacking the potency of facts, adjectives in most instances are hazardous unless they are used with great care. They can, for example, lead to redundancy. This is particularly prevalent in news writing. They can also be misleading. And they can very easily create the taint of editorial opinion in sentences intended to be purely reportorial. This is definitely not the kind of "color" we are seeking.

You will have no trouble finding sentences in which adjectives have been *combined with pertinent details.* Nearly always these are redundant sentences; adjectives rarely are needed if the facts are there. Sometimes this combination can be absurd: "The *hulking* six-footer weighed 267 pounds before his illness." Or: "The home team lost the twinighter through a *costly* error when Ellis dropped the fly." Another: "The 450,000 PTA members were urged to throw their *considerable* weight behind the proposed legislation."

Likewise redundant are such common adjectival phrases as "*exact* replica," "*foreign* imports," "*new* track record," or "*armed* gunman."

An erroneous impression results when adjectives are misplaced in the sentence: "The *treacherous* twenty-six-mile Arkansas downriver race will be run Tuesday." Since the river, not the race, is treacherous, the statement is misleading. The reporter should have written: "The twenty-six-mile race down the *treacherous* Ar-

*UPI Reporter, May 4, 1961.

kansas River will be run Tuesday." By the same token, the phrase *"unfair* labor practices strike" fails to make clear which is unfair— the labor practices or the strike.

You will recall (chapter II) that we have already met this fault of saving a very few words at the expense of *meaning*.

Factual documentation is the best way to avoid the hazard of slanting a story. Opinions (and adjectives so often reflect them!) belong on the editorial page or in the commentator's signed column. But they creep into newspage accounts when (a) adjectives are injudiciously included in descriptive sentences or (b) when such adjectives are not fully supported by facts. "When nonstriking workers report to the plant tomorrow, they will face a *challenging* line of pickets" is an editorialized assertion because the adjective implies a threat not yet within the realm of reality; it produces a sentence definitely derogatory to one of the two groups involved in the dispute. Without the adjective the sentence would provide an equitable forecast of the situation.

"De Gaulle sent his military commander, a *blistering* cable" likewise is an editorial sentence. But, unlike the preceding example, the adjective is not wholly to blame. The cable may very well have been "blistering," but unfortunately none of its text was included in the dispatch from which the sentence has been excerpted. Quite obviously, the content of De Gaulle's message was not released. The reporter nonetheless employed a colorful adjective in an effort to heighten the impact of his account. Had there been available to him any *factual substantiation,* his use of the descriptive word "blistering" would have been quite proper and fair as well as effective. But without the facts, or at least some of them, the adjective becomes an opinion word.

It is easy to see that any tendency toward editorializing can, if extended, lead to something far more dangerous—the threat of libel. Anyone can recall offhand at least a dozen adjectives—or verbs—heavily weighted with damaging implications.

Good Usage of Color Words

At the beginning of this chapter we endeavored to delineate the shortcomings of certain adjectives: most abstractions (such as "fabulous," "horrible," "vivid") are far weaker than facts; some can mislead; others may create redundancies or slant a story editorially. It would be a serious mistake, however, to conclude that *all* are therefore to be avoided. *Descriptive* adjectives ("purple," "leathery") are highly useful tools when properly handled. They enable the reader-listener to *visualize*.

The same may be said for various other parts of speech—adverbs, descriptive nouns, strong verbs—which help to create a word picture. Consider this passage from a United Press International story about the Adolf Eichmann trial:

> Hausner, a small, hawk-faced, baldheaded man in a black legal gown, faced the defendant with both hands on his hips. An angry flush appeared on Eichmann's ashen-gray cheeks as the prosecutor pressed his attack.
>
> A nerve in Eichmann's jaw twitched and he licked his lips nervously between questions. His voice rose angrily as he answered some of the more pointed questions.

Color elements abound in this passage. Let's list them:

Adjectives: Small, hawk-faced, baldheaded, black, legal, angry, ashen-gray, pointed.

Adverbs: Nervously, angrily.

Descriptive nouns: Flush, cheeks (more provocative than "face"), attack.

Verbs: Pressed, twitched.

Small details (facts): both hands on his hips, angry flush appeared, a nerve in Eichmann's jaw twitched, licked his lips, voice rose angrily.

Adjectives in their proper place. The late Stanley Walker, ebullient City Editor of the New York *Herald* from 1928 to 1935, told his newsmen to "pick adjectives as you would pick a diamond or a mistress."

Walker was stating what most veteran reporters learned long ago: writing that might be dubbed "lively language"—or, more sedately, "descriptive prose"—does not spring from the use of general words such as "exciting," "dramatic," "spectacular." Rather, it involves the use of precise wording and *exact detail.* And frequently it utilizes so-called color words that evoke visual images.

References to physical appearance or personal characteristics require just such specific description to be meaningful, and here the adjective frequently comes into play. The AP, in its obituary of actor Charles Laughton, referred to him as "the *plump,* admittedly *homely* screen veteran." UPI, telling about the death of Louisiana Governor Earl K. Long, described him as the *"madcap* last of the *red-hot* papas." A Washington correspondent, on a recent anniversary, wrote: "There, fifty years ago today, stood Woodrow Wilson, the *lean, lantern-jawed* college professor turned President, urging Congress to get started on his 'New Freedom' program."

A word should be said here about a special group of adjectival phrases which are in such general use that they have lost most of their potential threat of exaggeration. A casual reference to "summery weather" does not require bolstering with the precise temperature reading. Other examples are "criminal complaint," "increasing tension," "uninhabited swamp." In chapter II it was pointed out that many trite phrases have become so completely absorbed in everyday language that they have ceased to be clichés. Consider, for example, "How are you?"—"Good morning" —"Take it easy." The adjectives cited above are in much the same category.

Adverbs and descriptive nouns, valuable color words in themselves, often occupy the same sentence with effective adjectives.

"A *tired* tropical storm eased *gently* into Texas today" combines the telling use of an adjective, an adverb, and a happily chosen verb ("eased"). A descriptive noun and an adjective brighten this phrase: "A *swarm* of *pipsqueak* planets."

Forceful, active verbs are immensely helpful in capturing, and holding, the attention of the reader-listener. There is, in fact, a sizable school of news writers who believe that the verb is the most important element in colorful writing. In any case, there is no doubt that many provocative sentences gain their "punch" directly from the writer's choice of appropriate verbs. These must be precise as well as active and forceful.

However romantically he may have regarded *really effective* adjectives (p. 89), Stanley Walker held an even higher opinion of verbs that move:

> "He [the young man fresh to journalism] must learn, if he doesn't already know it, to avoid adjectives and to swear by the little verbs that bounce and leap and swim and cut."

For literary exercise, write down in one column as many commonplace verbs as you can think of. Then, opposite each, write the synonymous verbs which are more graphic or less ordinary:

> To face——Dare, challenge
> To press——Squeeze
> To decrease——Shrink
> To oppose——Combat, fight, confront

Many writers rob their sentences of action and force by employing one or another form of the verb "to be," or by combining some of these forms with other verbs. The moving, "working" verb is always a better choice in news writing.

The late Meyer Berger of *The New York Times* was a master of using the right verb at the right time. His fast-moving story about the Unruh killings in New Jersey in 1949 employed verbs like these:

"The tear gas was taking effect and police bullets were *thudding* at the walls around him."

"The druggist, still running, *bounded* off the roof and lay dead in Thirty-second Street."

"The little boy's head *pitched* toward the wound, his hair, half cut, stained with red."

"Men and women *dodged* into open shops, the women shrill with panic, men hoarse with fear."

Berger won a Pulitzer Prize for his readable account, which has been reprinted many times.*

Here are other examples of verbs that lured the reader as he progressed through a story:

The blast *whooshed* through the labyrinth of tunnels. An icy wind *whipped* the coal dust through the air.

An exposé that *jolted* the chief of police out of office.

Eight armed white men *yanked* the twenty-four-year-old Negro from the hospital cot.

Valentine's Day *laced* the Rochester area with a sweetheart of a snowstorm punctuated by thunder and lightning.

The nation's capital *heaped* a conqueror's honors today on a general who lost a battle.

Forty elephants *galumphed* briskly into town in the chilly early hours yesterday.

The date *snapped* out and Ferdinand Pecora *cracked* a fist into his hand.

A youthful Pennsylvania parole violator *twisted* himself into the arms of FBI agents at the Miami Police Athletic League auditorium yesterday.

Eleven Vassar girls *curtsied* today to an eight-man Sienna team, 14–6.

Astronaut Walter M. Schirra, Jr. *whirled* around the world six times today.

Attorney General Robert Kennedy, who occasionally *moonlights* as an auxiliary Secretary of State . . .

*See John Hohenberg, *The Pulitzer Prize Story*, (New York: Columbia University Press, 1959), pp. 118–128.

X15 pilot Joe Walker *shot* a record forty-eight miles into space today and came back boasting: "I could take orbit with no strain at all."

UPI said astronaut John Glenn came home to *"laughing, crying, cheering, pushing* acclaim from his country and his President."

Figures of Speech

The judicious use of simile and metaphor.   Miss Emily Pruitt, the legendary eighth-grade English teacher of innumerable newsmen, would sparkle with pride if she could read now the "compositions" they wrote as graduates. Although her lecture on the simile may have been long and boring, it ultimately produced sentences like this:

> The British light cruiser Galatea, struck by three torpedoes from an Axis submarine, flopped over *like a stabbed turtle* and went down within three minutes off Egypt's Mediterranean coast in the inky darkness just before midnight today. (Associated Press— Laurence E. Allen)

> The rocket stood there, minute after minute, with fumes of liquid oxygen drifting from it *like steam from a simmering kettle.* (Associated Press—Vern Haugland)

Nothing, perhaps, dresses up a story more effectively than the well-conceived figure of speech. Its principal asset is a sense of *propriety;* a simile or metaphor which *naturally* belongs in the context will, invariably, heighten the color of a sentence:

> U. S. Open champion Jack Nicklaus, *playing with all the emotion of a man mowing the lawn,* tucked away golf's $60,000 Tournament of Champions Sunday with a final round 3-under-par 69 and a 72-hole total of 273.

> A deflated balloon, which scientists had hoped would set a new altitude record, *fell like a giant teardrop.*

The good metaphoric sentence flows rhythmically:

The heavyweight championship dreams and claims of Nino Valdez and his slightly articulate manager Bobby Gleason are in the nightmare class today. The massive Cuban was thoroughly beaten last night.

In general, the simpler, shorter simile is most impressive. Here, however, are two which carry their weight pretty well:

For the average man it probably would be a dreadful ordeal to have to recite grandiloquent, boastful remarks he made years before. But Adolf Eichmann, to the astonishment of the prosecution, read the excerpts without stammering, *as calmly as though he had just found an item of moderate interest in the newspaper and was reading it over the breakfast table to his wife.* (*The New York Times*—Homer Bigart)

It (a ballistic missile fired from a silo) looked *like a giant Roman candle shooting out of a tin can buried upright in the sand.* (United Press International)

Straining for Color

Those who write rapidly can't expect to reach for a figure of speech as they would reach for a book on a shelf. If a good one comes to mind easily during the process of composing the sentence, use it. Otherwise, think twice before manufacturing similes and metaphors or patching up half-formed conceptions. There is, after all, something spontaneous about the effective figure of speech. One of the AP's more imaginative science writers, pounding out a night lead, came up with this one in reporting a conference of psychologists: "Dreams are the free movies of sleep."

The inept figure stands out like a black eye. Unless the simile or metaphor blooms naturally, without forcing, it is best forgotten— or, in some cases, at least set aside for use on a more suitable occasion. Unfortunately, there seems to be a strong tendency among many reporters to work far too hard in the effort to achieve such window dressing.

Failure in the course of this obvious striving is most strikingly evident in that monstrosity known as the mixed metaphor. Consider one that is really homogenized:

> To reply to it one must fire a scattergun because there is no nail-on-the-head answer. One answer would only rattle the fringes of the poser, without probing the heart of the matter.

Only slightly less confused is this one:

> A *grass roots* farm proposal dredged from months of interviewing Nebraska farmers was *on the table* today to *kick off* a planning session of the conference.

But metaphors need not be hopelessly mixed to be inappropriate or even in bad taste:

> Bill Muncie, a stocky young knight with a one-way muscle in his throttle foot, rides out tomorrow in quest of the holy grail of speedboat racing, the Gold Cup.

Particularly unfortunate is the metaphoric treatment involving activities or situations which are completely unrelated. The incongruous and distasteful linking of highway tragedy with a sports event was masterfully achieved in this sentence, which should have been killed on the spot:

> New Jersey had a no-hitter going as the Memorial Day weekend auto traffic game was about to enter its final inning.

Similes likewise can be disappointing when the writer strives too obviously. The reader can almost see the wheels go round in the reporter's head as he grinds out this farfetched parallel:

> GEORGETOWN—There is a poignancy about this city like that of a young girl who skittishly tries on hats but has a baffling disease that will kill her.

It may be argued, perhaps, that the simile above is not ill conceived. But in that case the reporter should have preserved it for a more appropriate occasion.

This simile is so long and involved that it fully defeats its purpose:

> Here at Gonen the boundary [with Syria] is halfway up a ridge of rocky hills. Living and working here is *like cleaning the steps of the New York Public Library every day while a man with a grudge against you watches from the upper floor of a Fifth Avenue building.*

Human emotions and inanimate objects. Writers plodding through a forest of color images often fall into the trap of endowing inanimate objects and occurrences with human senses or emotions, as in: "The device *cheerfully* resumed vibrating." The sound issuing from a teakettle may be pleasing to the ear, but the kettle itself is neither merry nor morose. And we have all noted in news writing such clauses as ". . . an accident which saw the top of the car sheared off."

Color Through Contrast, Analogy

Contrast is an advantageous implement of color or humor when used to create an unexpected, but not too bizarre, atmosphere. By reversing a commonplace conclusion the writer sometimes can give his reader-listener a small but provocative shock. In a profile on a tattoo artist, AP staff writer Charles Maher wrote: "People go to him when they want to get something on their chest."

In the opposite manner, citing something universally known can be useful in descriptive prose: "The rockets will be painted red, white, and blue—*just like the mailbox down on the corner.*"

As a matter of fact, the very names of colors are analogous to "color" in writing. William Howard Russell, covering Bull Run, reported: "Clouds of dust shifted and moved through the forest and through the wavering mists of *blue* smoke. . . . I could see the gleam of arms and the twinkling of bayonets."

The Associated Press, in its booklet, "Writing for the AP," cites these examples:

> Rex Beach's description of the surf as the "wild *white* horses of the sea."

> The poet's image, "Fog crept over the city like a great, *gray* cat."

> From a Revolutionary War battle scene: ". . . rumbled down the line of *red*-coated infantry."

There are others:

> Rich, *ruddy*, recalcitrant, and just turned sixty-eight, ex-Teamsters President Dave Beck goes to prison tomorrow to start a five-year term which he says "won't get me down, not by a helluva sight." (Associated Press—Paul Wells, Seattle)

> Gypsy Rose Lee is putting on her *black* dainties again—for musical comedy instead of burlesque. (*Ibid.*—William Glover)

A color name is combined with the shock of contrast (church and boxing ring) in this sentence:

> A *yellow*-haired kid with a smashed nose and scalloped lips dipped his finger in the holy water font of St. Jerome's Church, crossed himself with the fist that killed Frankie Jerome and went to his knees on the cold marble to pray. . . . (United News—Westbrook Pegler writing about boxer Bud Taylor at the funeral of a fighter he accidentally killed in the ring.)

The analogy of a hiding place became an oft-repeated part of the long-running series of stories about Whittaker Chambers and the documents he concealed in a pumpkin on his farm. Roger Tartarian of UPI was the first reporter to label these the "pumpkin papers."

Rhythm and Euphony

Most newsmen probably would deny that they deliberately inject rhythm into their stories. Deliberate or not, prose such as this contributes directly to color because of its measured, almost metered, flowing quality:

> The moon still shines on the moonshine stills in the hills of Pennsylvania. (Associated Press)

> Like something brought in from the graveyard, Mrs. Jane Gibson, the pig woman, lay flat on an iron hospital bed between a doctor and a nurse in court today and croaked out how she had shuffled down DeRussey's Lane one night more than four years ago "when the moon was bright and pretty" and ran smack into the middle of New Jersey's most sensational murder, the Hall-Mills case. (New York *World*—Dudley Nichols)

> Against the gray October sky, the Four Horsemen rode again in legendary lore. Their names are Death, Pestilence, Hunger, and Fire. These are only aliases. Their real names are Stuhldreyer, Crowley, Miller, and Layden. (Grantland Rice)

Euphony stems directly from a *feeling* for words. Not all writers possess this quality, which is much akin to an ear for music. It entails a tasteful choice of words and a provocative arrangement of sentences.

Words relate to the atmosphere in these examples:

> Little Nellie Morse, an innocent, girlish horse, won the Preakness yesterday and the diamond stickpin, the Woodlawn Vase, the $34,000, and the watery cheers of thirty thousand diving Venuses and Adonises who went swimming with all their clothes on. Fourteen other horses—all males—also Preaknessed around the swamp. They were seeing Nellie home. (Baltimore *Sun*—Raymond S. Tompkins)

The funeral tread of honor guards marching to the measured beat of muffled drums guided the way yesterday through the still, *green* hills of Arlington National Cemetery to the final resting place of Sgt. Ernest K. Turner of Berwick. (Newhouse Newspapers' Washington Bureau—Dick Sarge)

While a feeling for words is largely innate, many writers have heightened this sensitivity by a simple process: (a) practice; (b) read, read, read. But this procedure must be pursued seriously and diligently. It is not as easy as it sounds. There are, in fact, a great many critics who hold categorically that the writer who lacks this feeling for words will never amount to much. They are correct at least to the degree that it takes some talent to *conceive* the right word and to *know* it *is* the right word for the purpose to which it is put.

Here is a sentence from a London dispatch:

Informed of the suicide, Christine Keeler burst into tears and *ducked* into seclusion.

"Ducked" is, possibly, precise in the sense that she may have ducked into a doorway to escape the press (although the story didn't say she did). But in a sentence depicting a tragic situation "ducked" is jarringly colloquial. Even "fled" would have been better. After all, atmosphere is part of colorful—and all other good— writing. In the mood of the quoted sentence, "ducked" is not the word the reporter should have selected. Verbs—as well as nouns, adjectives, and adverbs—can and should reflect the tone as well as the action of the story.

The AP's Eddie Gilmore was well aware of this when he wrote the following lead:

Miss Pauline Testo—who runs a flea circus—was *scratching around* today looking for performers.

His verb isn't elegant, but neither is the story. (The phrasing also is a bit corny, for which we offer no defense.)

It was suggested a few paragraphs earlier that appropriate choice of words and provocative arrangement of sentences are the prime sources of euphony. Choice of words is probably the most important factor and surely the most difficult. But sentence arrangement must not be overlooked in the development of a flowing story that incorporates the acoustic effect of words. Common sense decrees that not every sentence should be as short as we can make it. The length should be varied. For practical purposes in news writing, the greater number probably will be shorter sentences, since these are easier for the hurried reader to absorb. But a preponderance of short sentences produces a choppy, uneven style. Strive for balance. And be certain that the longer sentences are simple enough to be followed rapidly. Our typical reader-listener may be a bus driver, but he isn't a primary pupil learning to spell out the words. Neither is he a moron. Oversimplification and over-abbreviation breed dullness, and dullness is the kiss of death in the newspaper or newscast; it neither serves nor satisfies the reader-listener at any intellectual level. Readability must have variety, not monotony.

Summary

In condensing this discussion it can be said that five elements are primarily important in descriptive writing:

(1) *Facts*, preferably obtained firsthand, greatly enhance the *emotional appeal* of the reporter's account, the *atmosphere* of the occurrence he is recording, and the *graphic impression* of the people and things he sees and hears. Such facts may be very small *details* indeed, yet freqently they will carry more *impact* than (2) *color words*, although these (adjectives, verbs, adverbs, descriptive nouns) contribute heavily when properly employed. Similarly of great value, when truly appropriate and free from strain, are (3) *figures of speech*, (4) the use of *contrast or analogy*, and (5) the creation of euphony and rhythm by precise *choice*

of words and tasteful *arrangement of sentences* varying in length.

No one will be so brash as to claim that any specific combination of such elements or the use of any particular technique would produce a prizewinning news story. Unlike mathematics, good writing arises, as T. S. Eliot said, out of the "agonizing ecstasy" of creation. But we can say certain factors are involved in such writing and, to quote Mark Twain, we can declare with confidence that the difference between the right word and the almost-right word is the difference between the lightning and the lightning bug.

VI

Starting the News Story—
The Lead

A news lead—the beginning sentence or sentences that convey the essential meaning of the story—should capture the reader as well as inform him. The lead is a showcase. It sells the story to the editor, helps him to write the headline. It enables the reader to learn quickly what the news is about, inspires him to go deeper into the story or to jump to another column if the event carries no interest for him. If the news does appeal to the reader but the first paragraph discourages him, it usually doesn't matter how good the rest of the story may be.

In the words of one veteran newsman, a lead should not be judged solely by its news content but also by whether it has a teaser in it. For example:

> Newscaster Ted Meyers was working in a new medium but his delivery never was better. (He delivered a baby.)

Zeke Bratkowski, who makes a speciality of beating the Los Angeles Rams, has joined 'em.

A clubwoman suggests red light districts might be given the green light as a last resort.

Some of the suspenders on the George Washington Bridge have lost their snap and are being replaced.

Gov. George Romney's ambitious plan to revamp Michigan's tax structure is dead because you don't look for the end of the rainbow when you already have the pot of gold.

The modern news lead is a simple, precise, summary statement of the most important or unusual single fact in the story. Selectivity is the key. The writer should keep the reader in mind and prepare the lead from the reader's point of view. Present the most significant facts from the standpoint of reader benefit, reader danger or other reader interest, not merely from the reporter's or participant's standpoint.

A few decades ago a different technique was employed in writing leads. The reporter wrote one sentence that answered six questions: Who, When, Where, Why, What and How. He simply had to cram all that information into the first sentence, then proceed with the details. The lead still answers those questions, but it can do so in two, three—even five or six—sentences. Today the first sentence is snappy, simple, and succinct:

CHICAGO (AP)—Nine detectives ambushed four gunmen after a supermarket holdup Wednesday and killed three of them.

LOS ANGELES (AP)—A federal grand jury launched today a full-scale probe into organized bookmaking in Southern California.

NEW YORK (AP)—Soviet Premier Khrushchev said today "it's all right with me" if a Russian defector stays in the United States.

DALLAS (AP)—A gunman assassinated President Kennedy from ambush Friday with a high-powered rifle.

Even in the complicated story, simplicity is regarded as the appropriate approach:

NEW YORK (AP)—A fantastic rush to buy gold swept world financial centers today, forcing the price to unprecedented highs.

LONDON—The price of gold soared again Thursday on the London bullion market. (*The New York Times*)

The Perfect Lead

It sometimes is argued that the following lead is perfect or nearly so:

The cow jumped over the moon today.

The lead is short and it answers most of the key questions. It tells who, when, where, what, and how. Presumably, the following sentence would explain *why* the cow jumped over the moon.

Actually, that so-called perfect lead can serve as a model for other beginning sentences. For example:

John Foster Dulles died today.

Princess Margaret gave birth to a son today.

The eight-month-old steel dispute was settled today.

The Pig Woman testified today.

The Teamsters Union called a citywide strike today.

The perfect-lead format frequently works best for highly complicated stories. The beginner should call upon it when the lead he has written seems awkward or incomprehensible.

Refining the Lead

As the reporter prepares to write a lead, he should ask himself: "What does this story mean?" Then he should write the answer to that question in one sharp, clear sentence. In the words of Theodore Bernstein, the reporter must "distill and redistill the content of the story until he has the clear liquid of real meaning."

The opening sentence should be as direct as possible. Information not required immediately should be placed elsewhere in the story. The most frequent violation of this "rule" is unnecessary attribution in the lead sentence. When the first sentence states a fact or idea accepted without question by the reader, the attribution usually can be postponed to the second or third sentence. In the following examples, the italicized words could be placed in a subsequent sentence:

A bequest of $250,000 to the University of Oregon Medical School was announced today *by Dr. Harry K. Newburn, President of the University.*

The San Diego State College debate team won eleven awards last week at the Western States Championship Tournament at Stockton, *Dr. Murvin I. Jones, coach of the team, said today.*

Fifty students joined the College-Y during a recent membership roundup, *according to David Neptune, College-Y director.*

The Assistant City Attorney, David M. Manning, announced that the city has settled out of court a suit brought against it by an elderly man who fell into an excavation ditch.

In each of the above examples, the attribution would have provided a convenient way to begin the second sentence.

When the lead states an opinion, however, the attibution must appear in the first sentence. An opinion printed by itself might be regarded as a fact by the reader or as an editorial opinion expressed by the newspaper. Notice, for instance, the effect of the attribution in the following:

The Midland College football coach should be fired.

The Midland College football coach should be fired, a freshman panel member contended yesterday at the Weekly Forum.

A wire service once sent out a story that began:

NEW YORK (AP)—There are two kinds of snails: male and female.

One newspaper edited out the dateline and inserted attribution this way:

> There are two kinds of snails—male and female, according to the Associated Press.

The result, obviously, was ludicrous.

In this wire lead, the writer apparently had an attribution complex:

> The Corpus Christi *Caller-Times* tonight says it has been informed that Lt. Lee Miller of the Texas Highway Patrol says he has been informed that it had been reported that two of his men have captured John (Jake the Barber) Factor and two of his abductors near Harlingen, Texas.

The Unusual Angle

On most small newspapers, nearly everything written by local reporters appears in print. But on a large newspaper or in a major wire service bureau, every story turned out must compete with others for space. Consequently, professional journalists soon learn to spot and emphasize the unusual element in a news story; they put it in the lead to attract attention to their story as it is weighed against hundreds of other words that cross the editor's desk.

In larger cities a holdup or robbery is considered routine. One or more occurs nightly, so a report of such an event holds little interest or importance for the regular reader. But the method employed by the robber or burglar occasionally is unusual—so unusual, perhaps, that what might have been merely a routine story is carried in newspapers across the country. Here are the essential facts in some crime stories that received coverage because of the unusual element stated in the lead:

> A bank is held up by a short, elderly woman whose age is estimated between seventy-five and eighty.

A grocery is robbed by a twelve-year-old boy brandishing a gun powerful enough to fell an elephant.

A robber enters a tavern and says, "This is a stickup." But few of the patrons hear him because the jukebox is blaring dance music. He unplugs the jukebox and repeats his announcement.

A young man buys a package of cigarettes, hands the clerk a $10 bill, then scoops up the contents of the cash register and flees. His net take is $8. The clerk still has the $10 bill.

A bandit, caught shortly after his misdeed, stands 6 feet 8 inches and weighs 375 pounds.

A bank robber escapes on a bicycle.

Three men rob a hotel, then are stopped for speeding by a state patrolman. While he is writing a ticket, he hears on his patrol car radio a police broadcast about the holdup. He arrests the men.

A bandit is a luscious-looking blonde who victims say was as pretty as a movie star.

A gentlemanly holdup man kisses all the women in a store and shakes hands with all the men whom he just has robbed. Then he races out.

A young, nervous robber faints during a holdup.

A bandit dressed in a tuxedo holds up a skid row café.

Here are examples of actual leads that stressed the different or unusual angle:

Tranquility ran rampant in Elmsford last night. No accidents, no fires, no traffic violations, no wife-beatings, and no dog bites.

Fifty million Frenchmen can't be wrong. There aren't that many.

Attorney Donald Bringgold, tears streaming down his cheeks, read from the Bible Monday as he pleaded for Carole Tregoff, on trial with her lover, Dr. Bernard Finch, in the 1959 killing of the doctor's wife.

Howard Hughes, the eccentric industrialist whose passion for privacy makes Garbo look like a publicity hound, has won indefinite immunity from public gaze.

A pipe-smoking woman language teacher and a navy artillery captain have confessed auxiliary roles in the latest assassination plot against President Charles de Gaulle, informed sources said Saturday.

The Archbishop of Canterbury, primate of all England, is vacationing in a pub.

The happy people of Bali have happily cremated their dead monarch.

A motorist took a fire to the firemen today.
Stopped by police with word that his car was on fire, he drove to the fire station two blocks away.

A retired rear admiral was fined $15,000 today for failure to pay import tax on 504 bottles of liquor brought from Guam aboard an aircraft carrier.

Municipal Judge Frank Nottbusch will settle an argument over the speed a traffic-ticket defendant was traveling by riding in his tiny sports car with him.

A woman fatally stabbed her husband last night in a dispute over which to watch on television—President Kennedy or Lawrence Welk, sheriff's detectives said.

Former President Truman told Republicans today to "go to hell" if they want an apology from him for remarks about Vice-President Nixon.

A man bit a dog here Wednesday, police Supt. Bill Humphries said. The animal, a police patrol dog, bit back in self defense.

Sometimes the fact stressed in a lead can best be described as unexpected rather than unusual. The story in this instance involves an event that contradicts a stereotype. For example, most persons would expect a minister to practice—without reservation —the teachings of Christ. When one deviated from that expectation, the Associated Press wrote:

A Baptist minister, embroiled in a year-long argument with a couple in his church, refuses to turn the other cheek.
"I want them to leave," he says.

Here's another example:

> Roger Kensler wiped his brow in the 94-degree heat and called a plumber to thaw out some pipes.
> It seems Kensler, manager of a supermarket, had casually tossed some dry ice in a sink.

The average reader would expect miners trapped in a cave-in to react with fear, perhaps panic. When a group of miners was trapped for days in Champagnole, France, the UPI wrote:

> Nine French miners, entombed since Monday, 220 feet beneath a slipping hillside, played cards in semi-darkness Wednesday and awaited rescue.

What kind of music do you expect at a funeral? This lead starts with the unexpected angle:

> While the brass band played "In the Good Old Summertime" and "A Bicycle Built for Two," the gypsies paid final homage to their king Wednesday.

In the third paragraph of that story was another glimpse of the unexpected:

> Barefoot children darted shrieking about the cemetery, while men in shirtsleeves and women in ankle-length skirts laughed and chatted. Gypsy custom decrees that mourners laugh, not cry, at funerals to cheer the bereaved.

When a Florida constable campaigned door-to-door for reelection, he came upon a fight between a saloonkeeper and his wife. He had two bottles and she had a butcher knife. So the constable arrested them both. The lead was natural: it said that Constable James Powell went campaigning door-to-door for election yesterday and lost a couple of votes.

Importance of the Verb

As noted in the chapter on descriptive writing, strong verbs add zest and vitality to a news story. Frequently such a verb can be used in the lead to attract attention and to add strength to the beginning of the story.

Newsman Bob Considine frequently employs in his leads verbs that are just a bit different, that seem to jump out of the sentence as you read it. He wrote of an early atomic explosion, for example, that it was like slapping God in the face. We don't usually link the verb "slap" with the noun God. So when we see the two together, embellished by a simile, we tend to pay attention.

One famous lead on the homage paid at Washington, D.C., to General Wainwright when he returned from a Japanese prison camp in World War II, used the unusual verb *heaped:*

> The nation's capital heaped a conqueror's honors today on a general who lost a battle.

How dull the lead would have sounded if the reporter had used the verb *paid:*

> The nation's capital paid a conqueror's honors today to a general who lost a battle.

When Marilyn Monroe toured Korea in 1954, one wire service reporter wrote this lead:

> A long, low whistle echoes across the frozen hills of Korea today as Marilyn Monroe continues her tour in an area where the men outnumber the women 100,000 to nothing.

Although *echoes* is a commonly used verb, it sounds appropriate in that particular sentence. Somehow the image of the cold, desolate battlefields of Korea merges with the idea of an echo. Substitute *was heard* for *echoes* and the sentence loses something.

One lead remembered by graying editors across the country was written by Damon Runyon, who said:

> The Yale crew arched their backs like eight angry cats and clawed their way to victory yesterday.

Today some editor probably would throw back the lead, contending that the noun and pronoun don't agree. But he wouldn't change *arched* and *clawed*—two verbs that may never have been used before then to describe a crew race.

The late International News Service writer Karl von Wiegand wrote in World War I that he had seen a wave of Russian flesh *dash* against a wall of German steel. Let's try some synonyms:

> . . . Russian flesh *move* against a wall of German steel.
> . . . Russian flesh *meet* a wall of German steel.
> . . . Russian flesh *oppose* a wall of German steel.

Clearly, *dash* is a powerful verb in Von Wiegand's lead.

When two airliners collided over New York City in a snowstorm and plummeted into residential-business areas, both the Associated Press and the New York *Daily News* picked the verb form *groping* for their leads.

The AP said:

> Two huge airliners, *groping* through snow-shrouded skies for landings, collided and crashed into the city today with fiery devastation. At least 125 were killed.

And the *Daily News* with a later version:

> In the world's worst aviation disaster, two airliners *groping* through a snowstorm toward International Airport and LaGuardia Field collided over the city yesterday, killing at least 131 persons.

The beginner should be cautioned to avoid straining for a colorful verb in the lead. Some news stories don't lend themselves to such treatment. The serious writer should stop somewhat short of sports-page English with its *clobbered, smashed,* and *trampled.*

When a peppy verb does seem natural—when it is pleasing to the eye and ear—use it. When it isn't, don't.

The Quote Lead

Some editors ban news stories that begin with quotations. The rule shouldn't be quite that severe, for sometimes a quote lead is highly effective.

Many editors fear that a permissive view toward quote leads will result in too many. And their fear is justified to an extent. Three or four quote leads on Page One would indicate the entire staff was in a rut.

But there are times when the quote lead tells the story quickly and aptly. For example, one Hollywood comedian in his sixties, sued on a paternity charge by a movie starlet in her early twenties, was asked by a reporter what he thought of the accusation. The Associated Press used his reply for the lead:

> "At my age it's a compliment," said comedian X, 63, about a charge in Superior Court that he had fathered the one-year-old daughter of a twenty-three-year-old movie starlet.

On the twenty-fifth anniversary of Huey Long's assassination, one wire service began the story this way:

> "What are they building the scaffold for?" asked the bulb-nosed man in the rumpled suit.
> "They're building it for you, Huey Long."
> Governor of Louisiana for less than a year, Huey Pierce Long had come to a grim crossroads in his hectic political career.

The quote lead gets the reader into the story immediately. If the opening words catch his attention, he probably will continue. In the above example, the word *scaffold* arouses reader interest, and the question itself prompts the reader to ask, "Why are they building the scaffold?" So he proceeds and, perhaps, reads the entire story.

When a B-52 was unable to release an X-15 rocket plane in

flight, the Los Angeles bureau of the Associated Press began the story as follows:

> "It was like having a bomb under one wing," said an official today after a B-52 landed with a fully fueled X-15 rocket plane nestled under one wing.

And another from the Los Angeles bureau:

> "The police have no clues. . . . We are therefore free to offer you a reward without questions asked."
>
> Forest Lawn Memorial Park, a cemetery, thus made a plea today for the return of $100,000 in gems stolen . . .

In New York a gentlemanly robber entered a bar and said: "Good evening, ladies and gentlemen. This is a stickup." And that's how the Associated Press lead began.

Frequently a quote lead can be used on a second-day story after the basic news already has been told in the straight-news style. A second-day lead on a ten-year-old city boy lost eight days in the wilds of Yosemite National Park began like this:

> "I was worried some of the time, but I never was scared," said a ten-year-old city boy who . . .
>
> "I thought someone would find me. I knew they were looking for me when I saw a helicopter fly overhead."

The main fact in that story had been reported the previous day: The boy was found alive. The second-day lead answered a secondary question: What was his reaction to the ordeal?

Used sparingly, the quote lead adds variety to the newspaper or wire service report. The test is whether the quote itself is important or unusual. Will it attract attention? Does it tell the reader something he wants to know? If it does, the quotation beginning may be not only permissible but also appealing.

Another word of warning: the quote lead must, in addition to getting attention, give a strong clue to the nature of the story. When a grand jury in Los Angeles began another investigation of the activities of gambler Mickey Cohen, one wire service began the story:

LOS ANGELES—"What, again?"

By themselves, those two words are meaningless. Contrast that beginning with the lead on the same story by another wire service:

LOS ANGELES—The federal grand jury today undertook a new inquiry into the financial affairs of gambler Mickey Cohen.

The Question Lead

The question as a means of getting attention already has been mentioned indirectly. If a question lead begs an answer—that is, if the reader feels he absolutely must seek the answer—the lead has fulfilled a key part of its mission.

This lead was described in the *AP Log* as a "feature winner":

Are there persons living today who lived another life, in another body—perhaps in some bygone century?

Well, are there? If you're an average reader, you'd probably seek the answer.

Here's an example from the now-defunct New York *Mirror*, combining a statement with a question:

Little Joey Rizzuto is dead. Remember him? He was the happy seven-year-old who celebrated Christmas on Thanksgiving Day last year because his doctors said he would not live until the Yule season. The nation cheered Joey in his fight.

He fooled the doctors and lived on to enjoy the real Christmas, but leukemia proved too tough to beat. . . .

The question lead can get the beginner in trouble unless he considers all possible answers to the question. A lead in one high school newspaper inquired:

Has Miss Bandy done it again?

The implications are obvious. Did Miss Bandy fall down the stairs to the cafeteria? Or did she hold up the local jewelry store while roaring drunk following a picnic? Or . . . ?

The Shocker Lead

Occasionally, a news writer tries to shock his readers into noticing his story. For example:

> NEW YORK (AP)—Bang, bang, bang, bang, bang, and bang!
> Six shots rang out and the Wells Fargo truck carrying $45,000 through lower Manhattan screeched to a stop.

Despite the pun, the above is a "one shot" lead; that is, it can be used once and probably never again.

Here is another example:

> "Jump, Jeff, jump!"
> The shrieks of a North Hollywood mother were drowned out by a fast-moving passenger train late Monday as it bore down on a stalled auto in which a terrified two-year-old sat helpless.

The shocker lead has one major drawback: it tends to induce overwriting, embellishment of the information. The facts themselves, if related precisely and vigorously, usually supply sufficient shock to attract attention in such stories.

The Suspended-Interest Lead

In the suspended-interest story, the writer ignores—indeed, flouts—the so-called rules for writing leads. This type of story is characterized by a punch line at the end. The reader is led through the introductory and middle paragraphs as if he were being presented a highly condensed short story. He progresses steadily toward the climax, just as he would in a fictional narrative.

The suspended-interest lead must intrigue the reader but not reveal the punch line or surprise. Here is how the *Christian Science Monitor* handled one such story in the early 1960s:

> A certain young man perhaps thought that he was soon to become something higher than lieutenant in the U.S. Naval Reserve. But like many other hopefuls he recently got a ten-page letter from the retiring Chief of Naval Operations, Arleigh Burke, stating that the Navy was unable to promote him from his present rank.
>
> Yet the military mind is not without its sensitivity. Expressive of the Navy's deep concern for its personnel was a passage pointing out that many who have failed to win Navy promotion have nonetheless "achieved a stature in civilian life which ranks them among the leaders of the circles in which they move."
>
> Undoubtedly the Navy's handling of this situation reassured John F. Kennedy of 1600 Pennsylvania Avenue, Washington, D.C.

Notice how the *Monitor's* lead piques the reader's curiosity by beginning with the phrase "a certain young man." The reader reacts by mentally asking "who?" Then he continues, seeking the answer. The lead has aroused his interest, but it has not told him the story.

The second sentence heightens reader interest through contrast and a second question: the young man thought he would get a promotion but he didn't. Why?

The third and fourth sentences suggest that this young man may be an important person, but they don't tell who. Finally, the last sentence discloses the identity of the young man, answering the reader's principal question.

Note that the story does not identify Kennedy as the President of the United States or as the Commander in Chief of the Armed Forces. To do so would smack of writing down to the reader in this particular story.

Note also that the second question—why—never is answered. The reader is left to infer that the letter did not explain specifically why Kennedy was among those passed over for promotion.

This Associated Press story follows the same pattern for both the lead and the story structure:

SWEET BRIAR, Va. (AP)—Into the post office of Sweet Briar College for Girls came a postcard, addressed to Box 408, from a Southern school.

"Dear Box 408," it read. "I was just wondering what the holder of my box number at Sweet Briar looks like.

"As for me, I am tall, dark, and I drive an MG. I am a freshman. What do you look like? Where are you from and what class are you in?"

Out from Sweet Briar went the reply. It read in part:

"I am tall, too, and not as thin as I once was. My hair is white, and I drive a Buick. I was a freshman in 1896."

Post office Box 408 at Sweet Briar belongs to the president of the college, Dr. Meta Glass.

Again, the lead on this suspended-interest story prompts the reader to ask, "What did the postcard say?" The answer is given immediately, but the full impact and humor of the tale are saved for the final words.

Here is another illustration, slightly different though it follows the same basic format:

GREAT FALLS, Mont. (AP)—A justice of the peace, in sentencing a blind youth for attempted extortion, warned the eighteen-year-old Thursday he must learn to live by the rules of a "man's world of sight."

Justice Pat W. Callahan fined Glenn O. Chamberlin of Harlowton $100 and imposed a sixty-day jail sentence with all but ten days of the sentence suspended.

The youth pleaded guilty to attempting to extort money from a local businessman.

"I was just stupid, I guess," was the only explanation offered by the youth.

Justice Callahan told Chamberlin, "This court will not give you any special treatment because of your handicap."

Then the judge added, "You see as well as I do."

Justice Callahan also is totally blind.

In that example, the reader is interested from the beginning in what appears to be unusual treatment for a person so handicapped. Again, he progresses through the story to answer the question, "Why?" He gets that answer in the final two words.

The same format is used here:

> VISALIA, Calif. (AP)—When Alexander Sharick was eight years old, his father caught him smoking and offered him a $20 gold piece if he quit.
> "I've never lied to you, dad, and I'm not going to now," the boy replied. "I've been smoking for a year and I can't quit."
> But Sharick has decided to follow his father's advice now because "it's a filthy habit and it wasn't doing me any good."
> Sharick is ninety-seven.

Other examples of suspended-interest leads and the outcome of the stories:

> MOLINE, Ill. (AP)—Kenneth Seelye became the toast of Adams Hall at Northern Illinois University at DeKalb when his daughter, Kenlyn, a senior, wrote a letter about him.
> (The final sentence of the letter, praising Seelye for filling the child's home "with the thrill of life and love," explained that she was adopted.)

> A bus driver sneezed twice today and sent three persons to the hospital.
> (He rammed into a telephone pole.)

> HAVERHILL, Mass. (AP)—Police gave no publicity to the theft of a four-foot bronze statue valued at about $300 a week ago because they felt some honest man might return it.
> (The name of the statue was: "Diogenes and Lighted Lantern in Search for an Honest Man.")

> LYNN, Mass. (AP)—Mrs. Janice Ross Chalmers' big trouble began some three weeks ago.

(She couldn't determine which of her twin baby daughters was Kally and which was Kelly. Footprints at the hospital solved the problem.)

Two final examples are printed here in full:

> CORPUS CHRISTI, Tex. (AP)—A petite, winsome brunette in a topless swim suit won a bathing beauty contest Friday night.

Winning over 130 other contestants was Tera Hunsaker, who was crowned Miss Wading Pool.

Miss Hunsaker is seventeen—seventeen months, that is.

VANCOUVER, B.C. (CP)—The bearded man in the patched pants registered at a hotel here, then headed for the cocktail bar.

The bartender told him that the way he was dressed he'd better go down to the beer parlor downstairs.

So novelist Ernest Hemingway, just in from a bear hunting expedition in northern British Columbia, shrugged his shoulders and went up to his room.

Humor in the Lead

Professional newsmen know that humor is one of the most difficult writing techniques. Even the experts such as James Thurber and Robert Benchley are said to have worked and reworked their stories before they emerged as hilarious art forms. The newsman, with a deadline that is now—not next month—hardly has time for such rewriting. Yet some superb examples exist of newswriting with a funny touch. One of the best known, perhaps, was a one-sentence news story about the weather. It said:

Snow, followed by small boys on sleds.

Though not the "ha-ha" type of humor, it has caused many a twinkle over the years in the eyes of those who regularly read weather forecasts.

Here's another:

The million-to-one shot came in. Hell froze over. A month of Sundays hit the calendar. Don Larson today pitched a no-hit, no-run, no-man-reach-first game in a World Series.

An example that long has been retold in various forms:

The Centerville High School string quartet played Brahms last night. Brahms lost.

And while music is the theme:

A piano player, using his fists instead of his fingers, tapped out the opening bars of Beethoven's Fifth last night on the nose of a holdup man at a local night spot.

The gunman slumped to the floor and police took him away.

One from *The New York Times:*

The lead tenor in a prison quartet led the bass and baritone to freedom last September, but the FBI has arranged for a return engagement at the Kentucky State Reformatory.

Here are two stories printed in full so that the lead, in effect, is the story:

Mrs. Jacqueline Kennedy went water skiing again today. She fell twice.

GUANTANAMO BAY, Cuba—U.S. Marine sentries today repelled an invasion of this naval base by three scrawny red Cuban chickens. They said, "shoo."

Hugh Baillie, former President of the United Press, wrote a memorable lead on a prophet who predicted a world revolution would begin on a certain day. When a downpour hit New York on that day, the longhair, disheartened, reluctantly announced the revolution was postponed until tomorrow. Baillie's lead brought congratulations from across the nation:

NEW YORK (UP)—Revolution postponed on account of rain. Two revolutions tomorrow.

When Don Stull, a former Ohio AP sports editor, started a story about a report 175 Ohio bridges had collapsed in a year, he said:

Ohio is getting caught with its bridges down.*

*Two often-repeated leads never were printed. On a little boy being run over, a wire service man in Rome wrote: "Giuseppe Blank raced a steamroller across a street here today. Giuseppe lost." A UCLA law professor borrowed a quarter from a student and asked how he could get it back legally. The student filed suit against the professor in Small Claims Court. One newsman wrote: "Professor John Blank got his tort caught in a wringer today."

In Nebraska, a convict filed a motion for a new trial, a notice of appeal, a petition for appeal, a petition for a writ of habeas corpus, a motion to override a motion to strike the defendant's motion for a new trial, a poverty affidavit, a motion to be heard on a motion for a new trial, and subpoenas for witnesses. A UP staffer started his story:

> Edward Blank, serving time in the Nebraska penitentiary for burglary, threw the book at the judge today.

Writing the lead frequently is a beginning newsman's most difficult task. The more he writes, the easier they become. But even the beginner should realize that veteran reporters occasionally have trouble with the first sentence or sentences.

Perhaps this example will show conclusively how the proper choice of words can make a routine lead sparkle:

> A twenty-five-year-old Milwaukee woman admitted, police said Thursday night, that she set ten apartment house fires so she could see her boy friend in action as a fireman.

As rewritten:

> A twenty-five-year-old blonde admitted today that she carried a torch for her fireman boy friend—from house to house, police said.

ANALYSIS AND SUMMARY
Essentials of Good Leads*

It would be easy to assume, from the preceding pages of this chapter, that good leads are commonplace. But hundreds of

*The careful reader will note on the following pages references to material discussed previously (notably in chapters II, III, and IV). A brief review nonetheless is considered advisable here, because many of the points already considered take on added significance when related to leads.

newspapers offer daily evidence that most leads aren't as good as
they should be. The first consideration, of course, is: Will the lead
you have in mind conform to the nature of the story? Is it appropriate to the subject matter? Feature stories may or may not be
informative, in whole or in part. Their leads need not be packed
with facts, but they must grab the reader. On the other hand, a
flippant first sentence is the worst possible introduction to the report of a tragedy.

Because straight reporting makes up most of the writer's working day, the following nine basic qualities epitomize good leads
for stories embodying newsworthy events:

Informative. The newsworthy lead must be more than a clutter of words vaguely related to the occurrence, such as the following:

> The nation's weather pattern showed minor changes today.

This doesn't even tell us if the weather was good or bad. The
implication is that not much happened among the elements. Yet
the body of the story provided details of thunderstorms, hail, and
high winds throughout the Middle West. Equally uninformative:

> Archbishop Karl J. Alter of Cincinnati tonight formally opened
> the 19th North American Liturgical Week.

Brief. However significant the news may be, brevity in the
lead is always a recommendation. It is difficult, and manifestly unfair, to ascribe any precise limit of length, but it is wise to stay
within 30 words—about three typewritten lines—even though excellent four- and five-line intros turn up occasionally. Obviously
we cannot tell the entire story in one sentence; when we speak of
the brief, or quick, lead we mean that nothing in the sentence delays or hides the chief newsworthy fact. Other major facts may
follow, in a second or even third sentence. Now and then, in complex situations, a good summary lead will comprise three short
paragraphs. And some of the worst will cram all of the news
angles into the initial sentence.

Too many words at once can be confusing, even if the sentence is properly phrased. Almost any long sentence is harder to read than two or three short sentences, sometimes in separate paragraphs.* The following lead is needlessly lengthened by lesser details which could be used later, if at all:

> A southbound automobile drifted across two of U.S. Highway 11's three lanes in predawn darkness today and collided with a tractor-trailer just north of here. All four occupants in (sic) the car were killed.

As rewritten:

> Four persons were killed today when their auto drifted across a highway and collided with an oncoming tractor-trailer. (or truck)

A minimum of detail can establish a vivid scene, if you are worried about getting some color into a brief introduction:

> Five boys took one last romp in the Susquehanna River today while their parents prepared to go home from a picnic. Four of them drowned.

Clear. Brevity contributes to lucid leads because it discourages involved and confusing combinations of facts or sentence elements. However, there are other causes of obscurity, even in brief leads. Most of these, in one way or another, are traceable to the writer's failure to say exactly what he means to say and in the proper sequence. An earlier chapter illustrated how a brief and simple sentence can be both basically accurate and ambiguous. Applied to leads, an unhappy arrangement of words produced this example:

> An electrical fire in the home of Robert Mingle was extinguished today before any serious damage was done by the Rosedale Fire Department.

The wrong impression that the death penalty is involved could be obtained from this factually true but awkward lead:

> The matter of a last-minute stay of execution which could precede a new trial for two former Truman Administration officials is now before a federal judge.

*See chapter II.

Accurate. Accuracy is an obvious requirement, and leads that distort the truth usually are accidents. Such leads go beyond the facts—or do not include enough of them. Example:

A San Bernardino bankruptcy referee charged with embezzlement was acquitted in Federal Court today.

In this case three counts of embezzlement were charged. The jury's verdict was not guilty on two. But jurors disagreed on the third count. This meant a subsequent retrial or dismissal of the third count. Innocence had not been established clearly on the third count, and thus the lead went too far.

Inaccuracy, in other words, is usually a matter of degree, except in leads which are deliberately slanted or sensationalized. A reporter bent upon producing a sensational lead will permit his opening sentence or paragraph to imply something beyond, or less than, the intrinsic verity of the facts he cites. A case of accidental death or manslaughter thus can give the impression of premeditated murder, or a purely political situation can hint at subversion.

A story about a man backing out of a driveway will illustrate. The account carried this misleading—and dangerous—lead:

A Gardena truck driver killed his father-in-law today, then surrendered to police.

Analysis will show that most libelous leads result from the reporter's effort to heighten the impact of his opening sentence by ignoring necessary qualification.

Simple. Complexities in leads scare the reader away before he has a chance to determine if he is interested in what the story is going to say:

National Association for the Advancement of Colored People attorneys told the Supreme Court today that overt public resistance is insufficient cause to nullify Federal Court desegregation orders.

Specific. Some opening sentences are so general in content that the reader isn't certain what the writer is going to say. A lead is sure to be dull if it is no more than an abstraction, or label, devoid of available drama. The following example is a nonspecific label:

> A disturbance on the East Side today called out police reserves who made fourteen arrests.

Deep in the story were these specific details, any of them worthy of a place in the lead: a crowd of 150 Negroes assembled; plate glass windows of a supermarket were shattered; the store was looted of liquor and cigarettes; four persons were injured by flying glass; the white proprietor was critically beaten; a National Guard call-out was narrowly averted. The writer should have picked the best of these for the first sentence of a story that had all the aspects of an embryonic race riot.

Not even a label—because there is no clue at all to the story's import—is this lead:

> A Texas pediatrician has cast doubt upon an almost sacred tradition.

Direct. Inverted, or backed-into, leads bury the news, usually by delaying the action. This can result from setting the scene before saying what happened:

> Two firemen fought their way into a smoke-filled building where a boy was trapped on the second floor today and died of asphyxiation.

The main thing that happened was left to the very end. The lead is unsatisfactory for another reason: lack of clarity. It is impossible to tell who died unless we convert the phrasing to a direct approach:

> Two firemen were asphyxiated today while trying to rescue a boy trapped on the second floor of a smoke-filled building.

Active. Nothing takes the punch out of a lead more effectively than inactive sentence structure. Smaller, more provincial papers are the best hunting grounds for such constructions as "A crash took the lives of three . . ." (for "a crash killed three . . ."); "Dave Jones has been ordered to testify today . . ." (for "Dave

Jones will testify today . . ."); "The U.S. Coast Guard today reported the collision of . . ." (for "A yacht and a freighter collided . . .")

Objective. Leads must stick to the facts for reasons other than
basic accuracy. In controversial situations this means the facts on
both sides. A lead which states only one point of view may be
correct factually but it remains unbalanced nonetheless and thus
fails to inform fully and fairly. Such leads are seen frequently on
political and labor stories wherein some of the facts conflict with
editorial policy.

Also nonobjective is the lead which draws a moral conclusion.
Both editorializing and philosophizing are activities lying outside
the reporter's province.

These lead starts are editorial:

> Chicago's angry probe into . . .

> A beloved member of the newspaper fraternity ended his
> career today . . .

This lead draws a moral conclusion:

> Anthony J. Heyman, 23, of Detroit, has *proved* that *crime does
> pay*—if not very much.

Other Refinements

Related to one or another of the essential requirements are a
number of qualities that enhance the basically good lead.

Choice of words. Color, interest appeal, and action depend
upon choice of words. Many examples cited in earlier pages of
this chapter can be used to demonstrate the difference between a
good, but routine, lead and an outstanding lead. Here is another:

> Rafael Trujillo, Jr. failed to graduate today from the U.S. Army
> Command College, but he became Commander in Chief of the
> Dominican Republic anyway.

The news is there, along with interest created by the contrast between success and failure. The lead is brief, correct, clear, etc. In short, it is a fundamentally adequate first paragraph which any newsman could have written. But here is what one wire service writer did with it by choosing his words cleverly:

> Gen. Rafael Trujillo, Jr. learned alternately in a matter of moments today that he had flunked in school and succeeded in life.

By the same token, poor choice of words can make a lead ridiculous, as in the use of colloquialisms or sports jargon:

> Howard Chandler Christy, the noted illustrator, *took* fifty-two mackerel fishing on the *Viking II* with Capt. Carl Forsberg, out of Freeport on Monday.

Choosing the verbs that denote action is always a good way to sharpen a lead, or any other sentence, provided we choose them correctly.

Time element. The best leads should contain some reference to the time at which the event took place. A certain amount of care is necessary in selecting the position the time element shall occupy in the sentence. It can be obtrusive, even absurd, if misplaced. This is particularly true in the present vogue of using the day of the week instead of "today," "yesterday," and "tomorrow," a practice favored by papers depending upon teletypesetter tape:

> Tuesday Weld Wednesday signed a new contract to make four pictures. . . .

In some papers "today" is sacred and must appear in every lead. Too often this produces an awkward sentence; the writer has phrased it to accommodate "today" instead of telling directly what happened and when, even if he had to age his story by using "yesterday." The Hearst press for years tried to make every occurrence appear to have taken place "today." The result was misleading as well as clumsy.

Unfortunate placement of the time element can blunt a sharp lead or even change its meaning:

President Eisenhower brushed aside "whatever difficulties the Soviets may raise" to talks on nuclear suspension today and sped three scientists to Geneva.

Neither the talk nor the suspension was due that day. The reporter should have written:

President Eisenhower *sped three scientists to Geneva today*, brushing aside "whatever difficulties the Soviets may raise" to talks on nuclear suspension.

Needlessly pinpointing the time element merely delays the news. "At an early hour today" means no more than "today" unless predawn darkness is a factor in the occurrence. And some leads give the time element more attention than the news:

Preliminary hearing has been set for August 21 for three persons held on child desertion charges in the swapping of a five-month-old boy.

Wire service people, writing for all cycles of the day, find it necessary to use the time element for updating. This can be acceptable, if not carried to an extreme. To freshen the report of an event that took place last night it is common wire service practice to adjust the time element to other facts in some such way as this:

Police questioned four men today in their search for the killer of a widow whose bludgeoned body was found last night in her modest home.

Almost any lead can be better phrased if the writer will resist forcing "today," into it. Telegraph editors like fresh developments in second-day leads, but if there aren't any the alternative is a fresh approach—possibly an angle of the story underplayed or omitted in the prior cycle.

A device frequently effective in second-day leads is the reaction approach. This is nothing more than comment upon what was said or done earlier, but it serves to update the story:

Top Democrats today disputed President Johnson's optimistic view yesterday of the nation's economic position.

Attribution. The importance of this factor in leads depends, first of all, on the nature of the story: Is the occurrence or statement innocuous, or does it embody the potential of libel? Obviously, a lead is more graceful, and easier to write, if attribution can be delayed until the second paragraph. Furthermore, the lead that is almost all attribution or identification tells us nothing or very little about what is to follow:

> Joseph W. Mathews, curriculum director of the Christian Fund and Life Community of Austin, Texas, was the Danforth Religious Seminar speaker at the University of Iowa Tuesday.

> *The Atomic Energy Commission said* today that *a panel of experts has agreed* that detonation of a small nuclear device twelve hundred feet underground will not cause any damage.

Many newspapers hold to a general policy of delaying attribution. However, this can be hazardous in crime stories or political reports. As we have already noted in chapter III (p. 41), there is a considerable disparity in libel codes among the fifty states, and wire services have agreed that the safest place for attribution, in one degree or another, is at the top of the story.

By degree we mean that often the source can be abbreviated from full identification (name and title) to "a prominent churchman" or "police said."

Many reporters for local papers assume they are safe with a lead starting, "Dow Bingel told police today he shot his wife and two daughters to death because. . . ." However, if Bingel repudiates a confession, if a court holds that his statement was obtained under duress, or even if he merely claims he was misquoted, the story started that way has no true attribution whatever. The publication itself takes responsibility for the fact that Bingel said anything at all.

That is why many editors—including those of the Associated Press—insist that the police bear the burden of proof. Such editors would phrase the above lead this way: "*Police said* Dow Bingel told them . . ."

Undoubtedly such a requirement induces the great number of

"so-and-so said" leads to be found in newspaper and newscast copy. But it is wise to limit the so-and-so approach to potentially libelous stories and to those wherein the person making the pronouncement is as important as what he says, or more so.

More than one sentence. Long, cluttered leads come from writers who try to put the entire story into one breathtaking sentence. The cure: simply break the lead into two or more sentences, or save some of the details for positions later in the story. Example:

> The second-place San Francisco Giants took advantage of a ninth-inning error in the first game and a gilt-edged pitching performance by right-hander Ruben Gomez in the second as they beat the Philadelphia Phillies 3–2 and 2–1 tonight to move within one percentage point of the National League lead. (48 words)

Broken up:

> Second-place San Francisco beat Philadelphia 3–2 and 2–1 tonight to move within one percentage point of the National League lead. (20 words)
>
> A ninth-inning error gave the Giants the first game and gilt-edged pitching by Ruben Gomez won the second.

More than one angle. A lead doesn't have to be long to be cluttered. A relatively short lead which tries to cover two or more news angles can impede a reader, even if the angles are related. Mixing two sports delays the real news and tends to confuse the reader or listener in this example:

> Dan Orlich, 6-foot-4, 320-pound former Green Bay Packer footballer and current captain of the All-American Trapshooting team, won the Pacific International Doubles championship today with 99 x 100 and then posted 100 straight in the first half of a two-day 200-target singles tourney.

Unmixed:

> Dan Orlich, 6-foot-4 captain of the All-American Trapshooting team, won the Pacific International Doubles championship today with 99 x 100. Then he broke 100 straight in the first half of a two-day 200-target singles tourney.
>
> Orlich is the 320-pound former Green Bay . . .

Quotes in leads. A writer's determination to work a direct quote, or partial quote, into his lead can befuddle readers:

> A resolution expressing concern for the "apparent inadequacies in the program for Indian-Americans in such areas as reservations, poor living conditions and voting privileges" was adopted today by the National Conference of . . .

Such a quote makes a cumbersome lead. In most cases it is best to paraphrase the quote in the first paragraph and then, if necessary, use it verbatim and in context later in the story.

The gimmicky approach. This is sometimes effective ("The herd shot around the world . . ."), but there is also the "cute" lead in which the technique is unsuccessful. Misused, gimmicky leads can and do repel readers, or tell them nothing, bewilder them, violate good taste. A blurred lead, in doubtful taste, is this one:

> Harassed jaywalkers, come to Kalamazoo. You can skip about the streets as you like—unless you want to get killed or injure others—come next Friday.

VII

Obituaries: The Delicate Description of Life and Death

Lizzie Miles, a laughing, mountainous, born-and-bred Bourbon Streeter who belted them out for the jazz bands of Kid Ory, died today at sixty-eight.

Benjamin F. Fairless, a coal miner's son who became head of the huge U. S. Steel Corp., died Monday in his home.

Dugald Semple, vegetarian and naturalist who lectured on how to live forever, died in a nursing home Sunday at seventy-nine.

The famous, ordinary, the infamous—all become news when they die. The final chapters of human lives have become such copy since the first—and only—issue of the pioneer newspaper in America—the Boston *Publick Occurrences Both Forreign and Domestick*. In 1690 it reported a "very Tragical Accident" at Watertown in which an old man of "somewhat a silent and morose temper" was found hanged in a cowhouse.

A reporter often writes obituaries on his first day or hour of work. And he may continue to write them until he retires. Even if he specializes, the newspaper writer may prepare obits on persons known in the field he covers.

Obits—like other news stories—range in significance from a front-page lead article about Marilyn Monroe's death to a page 27 item about truck driver John Smith's demise. When Miss Monroe died, the world was interested. When truck driver Smith dies, his relatives, friends, and associates are interested. To them, the page 27 story about Smith may be more newsworthy than the page one account about Miss Monroe.

Unless the beginning writer takes a long look at some well-written obits, he may assume their leads and structures differ from those of other news stories. They don't.

Moreover, just as there is no *one* way to write a news story about a bank holdup, no single method exists for writing an obit. Consider, for example, these leads on the death of actor Clark Gable:

> Clake Gable, undisputed king of Hollywood for thirty years, is dead. (Los Angeles *Mirror*)

> The King is dead. (Los Angeles *Examiner*)

> Clark Gable died at Hollywood Presbyterian Hospital Wednesday at 11 P.M. (Los Angeles *Times*)

All are short, uncluttered, precise—and different. The *Examiner's* lead probably wouldn't have been appropriate outside Los Angeles, but it told the story in four short words in an area where "The King" and Gable were synonymous.

The Obituary Lead

The newspaper writer should seize upon the one fact, event, or characteristic that made the deceased person different from other human beings—then put it in the lead. Here are examples:

André Houpert, an early aviator who was said to have been the first man to fly over Mexico City, died Thursday in Flushing Hospital in Queens. (*The New York Times*)

Arthur R. Vinton, known to millions of radio listeners in the 1940s as "The Shadow," died Tuesday at his home in Guadalajara, Mexico. (AP)

Actress Janet Leigh's father was found dead early Saturday in his Beverly Hills insurance office, a half-empty bottle of pills and a note nearby.
Police Chief Clinton H. Anderson said Fred R. Morrison, 52 . . . (Los Angeles *Times*)

Paul M. Butler, 56, former chairman of the Democratic National Committee, died today following a heart attack. (AP)

Frank Fay, old-time vaudeville comedian whose greatest role was playing straight man to an invisible rabbit named "Harvey," is dead at sixty-two. (Los Angeles *Mirror*)

Alec Templeton, 52, concert pianist and satirist who rose to international fame though blind since birth, died at his home here Thursday. (CTPS)

If a person has lived an exciting life, the reporter should try to inject that excitement into the lead. For instance:

Al Jennings, said to have been one of the most feared of the bad men in the blazing youth of the Southwest, died at 97 Tuesday with his boots off. (Los Angeles *Times*)

Attorney Jerry Giesler, the last of the great defenders of the damned, died today. (Los Angeles *Mirror*)

Fritz Kreisler, one of the greatest violinists of the twentieth century, died Monday—old, enfeebled, leaving behind in the world of music only the fading echo of his great genius. He laid down his bow twelve years ago.
"I live in memories," he said a few years ago. . . . Bitterness was a companion in his final years. (AP)
Henri Charpentier, sometimes called the Toscanini of the kitchen spatula, died Sunday at his Redondo Beach home. He was 81. (Los Angeles *Times*)

Former Governor Earl K. Long, the madcap "last of the red-hot papas," paid with his life today for the greatest political victory he ever won.

Dr. R. U. Parrott said the sixty-five-year-old Long "just rolled over and died" under an oxygen tent. Long had been in a hospital since winning election to Congress August 23 over fantastic obstacles. (UPI)

Mrs. Woodrow Wilson, widow of the President who shaped the League of Nations, has died at the stately brick town house where she cared for her stricken husband until his death in 1924. She was 89. (AP)

Occasionally, circumstances surrounding a person's death merit attention in the lead. When an elderly man died while dancing the twist, the Los Angeles *Mirror* said:

A seventy-nine-year-old man dropped dead, apparently of a heart attack, Tuesday night as he was doing the twist with 500 others in a ballroom at 1024 S. Grand Ave.

He was Bernard Tamplin, a real estate broker. . . .

Other examples:

An aged Glendale man died at the wheel of his car Friday after being told he had failed the driver's test for renewal of his license.

Robert Galbraith, 80, of 414 Thomas Ave., slumped over his steering wheel in front of the Department of Motor Vehicles office seconds after the inspector stepped from the car. (Los Angeles *Times*)

I. G. (Ike) Morgan, 56, vice president of Texaco, Inc., and chief executive officer of the company here, collapsed and died Thursday while addressing an oil industry meeting in the Statler Hilton. (Los Angeles *Times*)

Playwright Moss Hart died of a heart attack today as he was getting into his car with his wife, actress Kitty Carlisle. He was 57. (UPI)

Sen. Robert S. Kerr, D-Okla., one of the Senate's biggest men in both size and influence—and reputed to be its wealthiest member —collapsed while talking to his doctor Tuesday and died minutes later. (AP)

Hanns Ditisheim, 59, venturesome Swiss-born financier with a taste for the daring big deal, took the last plunge of his colorful life early yesterday from the roof of a 17-story building in the Bronx. (New York *Daily News*)

As the Washington *Post* tells its newsmen: "Next to the very fact of death itself, there is usually no news element in an obituary story as interesting to readers as the cause of death." * Frequently the lead contains that information:

A. Whitney Griswold, 56, president of Yale University, died Friday of cancer at his home. (AP)

Boris Pasternak, 70, noted Russian poet, author of the controversial novel "Dr. Zhivago" and winner of the 1958 Nobel Prize for literature, died in his sleep last night.
He had been confined to his bed since May 1 with lung cancer, a heart ailment, and other infirmities, and for several days had been in a coma. (AP)

Actor-director Gregory Ratoff, 63, died here early this morning. He had been under treatment for a leukemia-type blood disease. (UPI)

Marilyn Monroe, blonde, beautiful, and bewitched, was found dead Sunday in the bed of her Brentwood home, apparently the victim of an overdose of sleeping pills. (Los Angeles *Times*)

Prof. Friedrich Sessauer, 81, internationally known radiologist, died here Saturday after a long illness caused by his years of X-ray experiments. (AP)

Bruno Richard Hauptmann walked into the Trenton State Prison death house today and sat down in the only unoccupied chair in the room. (Quentin Reynolds)

Post Script, April 1, 1963. It continued: "Recently our obituary pages reflect the disinclination of many families to give us the cause of death.
"This is a common and quite prevailing idiosyncrasy but one we ought to work at steadily to overcome.
"There are some causes of death that are invidious and that reflect upon the deceased or his family, but in the overwhelming number of cases this reluctance rests solely upon an old-fashioned superstition or false sense of reticence.
"Let us try to get the facts to the very best of our abilities so that we may convey to our readers a piece of information that will gratify a very universal human curiosity."

The State of New Jersey, which spent $1,200,000 to capture and convict Bruno Richard Hauptmann, executed him tonight with a penny's worth of electricity. (UP)

The Obituary Story

Most of the foregoing examples happen to embody the long accepted formula of the Five W's in the lead. However, this adherence to tradition is not mandatory; neither is it always the most effective way to start an obituary.

One illustration, used for many years by journalism instructors, points out how simplicity sometimes is the best technique in preparing a story following a person's death. A young reporter, aboard a train taking President Harding's body to his native state of Ohio for burial, was laboring over a lead sentence. What he wrote seemed too flowery or too complex. As he walked to the front of the car to get a drink of water, the young man happened to glance over the shoulder of a veteran reporter who had just clacked out a lead on the story. The sentence read simply:

Harding of Ohio came home today.

The technique has been used many times. One other well-known example occurred after a Texas school exploded, killing 450 students. As one newsman prepared to cover a mass funeral service for the youngsters, he wrote this lead on a precede:

They're burying a generation here today.

The body of the obituary should relate in lucid, precise language the highlights of the deceased person's life. No rule says that the obit must be as grim as the fact of death; nonetheless, many seem to be written as if the reporter had a heavy heart.

William Allen White, the fabled small-town editor from Kansas, is said to have changed his writing style when he heard two men laughing at vain, pompous phrases he had used in an obit. White had said:

> His name will be carved in the hearts of his countrymen and carved deep in the tablets of fame after the echo of other names will have died away and are lost forever.

Biographer David Hinshaw said White changed from a flamboyant to a simple style because of the incident.

Several writing devices can be used to show what the dead person had been like. Among them:

The well-remembered quip or saying.   When H. L. Mencken died, obituaries recalled that he once had said readers should not mourn his passing; rather, they should remember him by winking at an ugly girl.

The anecdote.   The AP's obit of violinist Fritz Kreisler told these two stories:

> Once he was hired to play in New York for a private party given by a wealthy society dowager. She asked him how much he would charge. His answer was $10,000. Then the matron said: "You know, Mr. Kreisler, that you may not mingle with the guests." His reply: "Well, then, madam, my fee is only $5,000."

> An old man once stopped Kreisler on a street in downtown New York and asked how one gets to Carnegie Hall. Kreisler replied in one word: "Practice."

Description of personal traits.   Although the following is from a eulogy of *The New York Times* reporter Mike Berger, and not from his obituary, it is a brilliant demonstration of how words can paint a picture of a man:

> The fun is gone from the city room. Sweet, gentle Mike Berger is gone. Unselfish Mike Berger, who signed more bad notes and gave up more soft touches than anyone else. Kind Mike Berger, who did more favors for scrubwomen and elevator operators, porters, copy boys, and even complete strangers, than anyone else would have dreamed of.

> Impish Mike Berger, delighting his fellow reporters with some wild, incredible yarn that always turns out to be true; rousing them

to great gusts of Rabelaisian laughter with some anecdote of his youth. Patient Mike Berger, sometimes doubled over his desk with pain from his stomach ulcers, but never, never complaining.

Mike was the master craftsman, never so happy as when he was batting out a big story under the gun of a deadline. . . .

When Jack (Doc) Kearns, manager of Jack Dempsey and other boxing champions, died in Miami, the Associated Press obituary used this quote:

"I've told so many lies in giving out stories that sometimes I don't know myself when the lies end and the truth begins," Kearns said several months ago in discussing his fantastic career.

The obit, pointing out that Kearns was a ballyhoo artist supreme, told this tale:

His stories were so fantastic they usually got him and his fighter space in the papers.

Once when Joey Maxim, who had lost the light heavyweight title to Archie Moore, was training in Miami for their third fight, Kearns ordered the gym cleared so "Maxim could practice his secret punch."

Maxim apparently hadn't been informed of this latest bit and when he saw Kearns waving his arms and ordering everyone out, he asked a reporter what was going on. Told about the "secret punch," Maxim broke up laughing.

"Me, secret punch," he said. "You gotta hand it to the Doc. I couldn't knock down a chorus girl."

In its obituary on actor Peter Lorre, the Associated Press referred to his "soft-boiled egg eyes and whiny voice," then added:

Lorre for years adhered to the principle of eating and drinking as one pleases—and absolutely no physical exercise.

Reporting the death of Nancy Lady Astor, the first woman to be seated in Britain's House of Commons, the Associated Press mentioned that she did not hesitate to use "the sharp edge of her tongue on any who displeased her."

The wire service recalled that Virginia-born Lady Astor once tangled with Winston Churchill, who described her entrance into the all-male Commons this way: "It was like being found naked in the bathroom with nothing but a sponge to protect you." The obit continued:

> Lady Astor once remarked to Churchill:
> "If I were your wife, Winston, I'd put poison in your coffee."
> And Churchill replied:
> "If I were your husband, Nancy, I'd drink it."

The final utterance.   When Vice-President Alben Barkley collapsed and died while making a speech, the press recorded the words he uttered just before he collapsed: "I would rather dwell in the House of the Lord than sit in the seat of the mighty."

As Frederick Charles Wood, a cocky, confessed killer of five persons, was strapped in the electric chair at Sing Sing, he said: "I really want to ride the lightning. Gents, this is an educational project. You are about to witness the damaging effect of electricity on Wood." His words described perfectly the type of man he had been.

Stories After Death

Sometimes the events that follow death are more unusual or significant than anything that occurred in a person's lifetime. Here's an example:

> In all his eighty-five years Walter Lavender never forgave the internal combustion engine for replacing the horse. He never rode in an auto.
> His granddaughter, Jill Cavanagh, told newsmen: "He once pointed to a motor hearse and said, 'I don't want to go to my grave in one of them. It isn't fit and proper.'" She added:
> "When he knew he was dying, he made my grandmother and me promise that we would get him a horse-drawn hearse."
> At first the family had no success. "There isn't an undertaker in the country who still uses horses," they were told.

But Walter will get his wish. A film company is providing four bays and a splendid black carriage to carry the horse lover to his grave today.

"We had thought," Mrs. Cavanagh said, "that if we couldn't get this hearse we might take him to the cemetery in his own cart, behind his old mare Brenda. But I'm afraid she might have been too frisky." (AP)

When a circus midget who had lived in Atlanta died in 1946, Frank Daniel of the Atlanta *Journal* wrote what is regarded by many as a classic lead:

A three-foot midget in a man-size world went to glory Friday in a six-foot grave.

And the final story about a man who had lived underground:

They buried Charlie the Mole yesterday in a cemetery not far from where his burrowing exploits startled the city of New Orleans. (AP, David Zinman)

When Lola Adams, the queen of the nation's gypsies, died in 1962, many newspapers reported her death. But neither the events of her lifetime nor her death approached the human interest drama that occurred in the days preceding and including her funeral. More than 250 of her subjects, brightly garbed, flocked to Los Angeles from all parts of the country. The Los Angeles *Herald-Express* wrote:

A gypsy band played a mournful dirge as the bronze coffin left the mortuary bound for a solemn high requiem Mass at St. Aloysius Church. Traffic was snarled for blocks in the area as wailing mourners, heedless of the rain, followed the coffin to the hearse.

Queen Lola, laden with jewelry and with money—both paper and coins—placed in her coffin, was taken to the cemetery with all the ceremony of a reigning monarch. Afterwards, the manager of the mortuary had this problem: the mourners had brought piles of the Queen's favorite foods so they would be available for her final journey, but many of the delicacies had been left at the funeral home.

But crowds aren't required to make a powerful human interest story. Here is a masterful example, written by the AP's Dial Torgerson, of a human being's final moments of life and her brief funeral rite:

Maureen Claire McLaughlin never met the last friend she had in the world.

He was a detective.

The first time Lt. Ernest Vandergrift saw her was the night of May 29. She was lying dead in a street near a liquor store.

The liquor store owner, Arthur Nelson, said she had tried to rob him and a customer at gunpoint. Nelson had whipped out his own pistol and shot her twice in the chest.

Her white sandals were in the door. She had run out of them in her terrified flight. Next to her was a white purse. There was no identification in it.

What had happened was clear. But what Vandergrift wanted to know was: Who was she?

She was very blonde, very young, and very pretty. Usually with dead criminals, identification is easy. Police records have long memories.

But this girl, strangely, had no police record. The FBI had no record of her fingerprints.

Coroner's aides suggested burying her as Jane Doe.

"No," said Vandergrift. "She should have her right name back before anyone buries her. It's only right."

Through tipsters, Vandergrift learned she had frequented bars on Hollywood's seamier side. Few of her male acquaintances would talk. (Six of them, through Vandergrift's efforts, now face possible grand jury action as members of the robbery ring the girl had joined.)

She was known by a variety of names: Eileen, Mary, Irene, Kitty. She came here from the East last spring, they said, looking for a job as a model. Instead, she found friends with the crowd —that shady segment which hangs out on the shadowy fringes of Hollywood.

Vandergrift worked night and day trying to learn her name. He took people to view her body at the morgue almost daily. Once he thought he had a positive identification, but it turned out to be false.

He missed a lot of meals at home. But he continued his investigation.

Then, last week, two clues paid off.

The mother of a young man the girl had dated remembered that she had said she had bought an insurance policy before leaving Cincinnati, Ohio. And the mother remembered her using the name McLaughlin.

After 45 days, Vandergrift closed his case: The girl, he announced, was Maureen Claire McLaughlin, daughter of Harry McLaughlin, a professor at the University of Cincinnati.

Thanks to insurance company records, the identification was positive.

She would have been 19 yesterday.

Tuesday, under her right name, they buried Maureen at Valhalla Memorial Park—ironically enough, two blocks from where she was killed.

Her father, reported in ill health, didn't attend. There were no mourners.

Sometimes events following death take a strange—perhaps unique—course. Consider, for example, this UPI story:

W. W. Tunnell, who died six weeks ago, was elected Democratic chairman of Precinct 35 in Tyler, Texas, in Saturday's primary election.

Tunnell defeated C. W. Sessions, Business Manager for the International Brotherhood of Electrical Workers, 228–117.

Conservative Democrats campaigned vigorously to get Tunnell elected so when the Smith County Democratic executive committee names a replacement for Tunnell it will be a conservative.

Or this lead on a San Diego man who failed to accept the fact that his only son had been killed in World War II:

Thomas E. Sharp, wealthy San Diegan who died last November, left half of his fortune, estimated at $28 million, to his dead son. (San Diego *Tribune*)

Another example:

A divorce court judge in London ruled today you can't divorce a dead man.

Judge Sir Jocelyn Simon decided in the court that a decree against a dead man is a nullity. He said:

"A man can no more be divorced after his death than he can be married or sentenced to death."

He set aside a decree granted to Mrs. Florence Heanan in an undefended case last December on the grounds of her husband's desertion. The husband, David Heanan, died in September after being served with legal papers initiating the action.

The judge said Mrs. Heanan applied for the decree to be set aside because she wished to retain her widow's rights. He said anyone affected by an order which is a nullity is entitled to have it set aside. (AP)

Wills, of course, often are more newsworthy than anything their writers did while alive. One will filed in Los Angeles attracted considerable attention when the court couldn't decide if a punctuation mark was a comma or a period. The amounts that would go to the two beneficiaries hinged on the answer.

Another will filed for probate in Los Angeles left specific sums to the dead man's sons if they married women who met certain intellectual and physical qualifications. The dead man, a student of eugenics, wanted to produce "superior" grandchildren. The AP's Joe Lewis wrote this lead to the story:

> A Harvard psychologist who died after a lifetime devoted to studying the human race has left a will designed to improve it.
>
> Method: cash bonuses for his two sons.
>
> Condition: they and the wives they select must score well on a series of mental-physical character tests.

In London, a housewife used 95,940 words to write her will.

Robert S. Menchin, in his book *The Last Caprice,* tells about a man who disinherited his two sisters because they had voted for Franklin D. Roosevelt. And a Frenchman, says Menchin, left his estate to a lady who had refused to marry him twenty years before, resulting in what he termed a happy bachelorhood.

One will stipulated that the dead man's son-in-law would receive fifty cents "to buy a good stout rope with which to hang himself."

Some Supplementary Hints
on Writing Obits

Accuracy.   One of Joseph Pulitzer's best-known dicta, "Accuracy!
Accuracy! Accuracy!," should serve as a motto for the obit writer.
If an obit is inaccurate, descriptive—even brilliant—writing will
be overlooked.

Relatives and friends of deceased persons will spot inaccuracies
quickly—and they frequently will tell the city editor about them.
Unlike other news stories, obits are clipped and saved by relatives. They should be correct.

Check the clips.   Although many sources exist for information
about a person who has died, a reporter always should check the
newspaper library for clippings about the deceased.

This obituary, printed here in full, appeared in the Seattle *Post-
Intelligencer:*

> Miss Evelyn Jones, 73, of Wesley Gardens, died Monday at
> West Seattle General Hospital.
> She was born at Red Wing, Minnesota.
> Survivors include a sister, Mrs. Nona Larrabee, Seattle, and
> two brothers, Dr. N. W. Jones, Saratoga, California, and P. E.
> Jones, Kelso.
> Funeral services will be held Friday at the Bonney-Watson Co.
> Cremation will follow.

After the obit appeared in the first edition, a friend called and
told the city desk that the income from the half-million dollar
estate of Miss Jones' brother was to go to the University of Washington Medical School upon her death.

"You ran a story about it several years ago," the caller said.

Clippings in the newspaper's morgue, of course, told the entire
story. They hadn't been checked by the reporter.

The second edition carried a two-column story about Miss Jones on page one. The lead read:

> One of the largest bequests ever made to the University of Washington became effective yesterday with the death of Miss Evelyn Jones, 73. Upon her death, the income from the half-million-dollar estate of her brother, Dr. Everett O. Jones, goes to the University Medical School to be used for student loans and grants.

Synonyms for "dies." Some newspapers permit the use of terms such as "passes away," "passes," "succumbed," "death claimed," "departed," etc., as synonyms for "dies." These words, however, sound too heart-rending to many editors. The word "dies" is short, precise, and most meaningful—facts that justify its use in most obits.

Wife or widow. Roy H. Copperud, a California journalist and a columnist for the trade magazine *Editor & Publisher*, says a war may be fought someday between newsmen who hold that a man is survived by his *wife* and those who insist he is survived by his *widow*.

"Stylebooks," says Copperud, "favor both sides of the argument."

His own preference inclines toward wife. However, effective arguments can be made for either word. Perhaps a swift way to settle the problem is to adopt the wire services' preference for *widow*. Or ask your city editor for his opinion.

Age. A person's age tells more about him in a smaller space than almost any other type of information. Yet survivors often are reluctant to disclose a relative's age. The reporter should explain that neither relatives nor the dead person can possibly be affected by printing the age. When politeness fails, newsmen sometimes have resorted to subterfuge, such as deliberately telling the survivor that the newspaper has information that the deceased is such and such an age. Presentation of a hypothetical figure occasionally has prompted a survivor to reveal the true age.

Profession. A reporter should make every possible effort to determine the dead person's profession. Frequently it is the most interesting fact in obituaries. If he was a fish cleaner at the Front Street market, say so in the obit. This may tend to create a stereotype in the reader's mind, but it also tells much about the person. If he was a fish cleaner who wrote scholarly articles about Keats or Thoreau, then you've got an even better story.

Nicknames. If used, nicknames should be placed in parentheses, such as Herbert (Joey) Flaggin. Most editors discourage the widespread use of nicknames for the simple reason that every person is entitled to die with dignity. Exceptions occur when notorious criminals die. They often are better known by their nicknames, such as Joe (The Enforcer) Ketchum.

Addresses. Obituaries should give the person's address. It helps answer one of the key points of the lead: Where?

Of-from. A person dies *of* a disease or ailment, not *from* it. ("House Speaker Sam Rayburn died of cancer today.")

Sources. Mortuaries usually prepare a death report on persons. The reporter can get most of the basic information about a person from the report. This can be supplemented by data obtained from relatives, friends, associates, employers, and, of course, clippings in the morgue.

Body. A body is presumed to be dead. The term "dead body" is redundant. Moreover, the body may be *sent* someplace for burial, not *shipped.*

Once the fact and circumstances of death are established, the obituary deals with *life,* not death. It should be a precise, accurate, well-written mirror of that life. And remember to write for the reader—even those like lawyer Clarence Darrow who said: "I have never killed anybody but I have read a lot of obituaries with relish."

VIII

Feature Favorites

A strongman bends a steel bar around a girl's neck, then can't unbend it.

A weather forecaster is fired for being inaccurate.

The pockets of a dead skid row derelict yield a few coins, a handkerchief, and a Phi Beta Kappa key.

A man named Donald Partridge tries to fly like his namesake. He fails.

Ice cubes fall into a Southern California backyard on a summer afternoon.

Such is the nature of feature stories—those often whimsical, sometimes solemn mavericks of the newspaper page. There are no rules for writing them. They fit no neat pattern. A successful approach and format for one may prove ineffective for another.

Saul Pett of the Associated Press has described feature stories this way:

If the story makes you or your wife or your laundryman laugh or cry or say, "Well, I'll be damned" or "By gosh, that's just how I feel" or "It could happen to anybody" or any of the countless ways of saying "It's a small world"—if the idea moves you or your friends to any of those reactions and it's likely to have the same result among enough people beyond your own state, then clearly you have a good national feature story.

Pett's colleague, Hugh Mulligan, categorizes feature stories and offers this waggish example:

If a man can build another Taj Mahal out of toothpicks, that's a good local feature. If he makes it out of toothpicks while lying in an iron lung, that's a state feature. If he does all this while his wife keeps running around unplugging the iron lung, that is a national feature.

The writer who can evoke a response such as laughter or tears always has been and still is a rarity. In most cases, he is a trained craftsman with lengthy experience as a reporter of straight news. In all cases, he combines a flair for descriptive writing with the intellectual stamina to work long and hard over a single idea. He is a polisher, searching for the precise noun, the razor-edged adjective, the powerful verb, and the bouncy adverb. And he is a builder, weaving facts and color into a pattern that compels the reader to continue.

What Is a Feature?

There is no one definition for a feature story. It may differ markedly from a straight news story, or it may contain much hard news. In general, however, these characteristics tend to distinguish features from more routine, straight stories:

1. A city council story on zoning law changes is stale news if its publication is delayed a day. But the time element usually is of

little importance in a feature. Whether it is humorous or carries an emotional wallop, an effective feature can wait for tomorrow's editions. Exceptions, however, are features pegged to the news, such as the personality sketch, the backgrounder, or a local reaction piece. These timely sidebars should accompany the hard news account.

2. Features frequently are funny; in fact, many exist solely because of their humor. Although straight news stories may indeed include humorous facts or a witty writing style, these qualities are incidental to the main point of the article.

3. Newsmen often must seek out the feature aspects of an event, whereas its news impact may be obvious. The trained feature writer has learned to sense immediately the unusual, humorous, dramatic, or sad elements in an occurrence. The inexperienced reporter may readily see the news angle but fail to recognize the feature aspects.

4. A reader identifies more quickly and more personally with a feature story. He may be amused or depressed. He may be saddened or infuriated. In a sense, he becomes a vicarious participant —one who says, "Why, that's happened to me" or "I'm glad that hasn't happened to me."

5. A feature story often ends with a punch line—a strong final sentence that carries the reader back to the lead and wraps up the story in a tidy package. In this sense it tends to resemble the short-story format.

One way to distinguish between features and straight news stories is to examine both approaches when they involve the same general subject. The fact that two astronauts returned safely from an eight-day trip is hard news. What they ate and how they ate it is feature material. The fact that a long-stemmed beauty from Georgia won the Miss America contest is hard news. What her seventeen-year-old sister thought about it is feature material. The fact that the FBI captured one of its ten most-wanted criminals is hard news. The spadework that led to the arrest is feature material. In short, the immediate, significant aspects of an event are reported as straight news. The peripheral, less important aspects may supply the grist for a feature.

Here are some examples of the type of features offered in recent years by the Associated Press:

Jules Loh wrote a discerning profile of Mississippi, "where a soft breath of change" was being felt.

Sid Moody prepared an in-depth study of the population explosion.

Hugh Mulligan offered a lively portrait of Sen. Russell Long— the son of Huey, the nephew of Earl—when he became the new Senate majority whip.

W. B. Ragsdale, Jr., examined the Peace Corps, which at a young age was "worrying about hardening of the arteries."

Tom Henshaw wrote a humorous profile of the "world's best-known party pooper," the Boston censor Dick Sinnott.

As Don Duncan, feature writer for the Seattle *Times*, puts it:

> A feature offers a fresh approach: A way of capturing the pathos, drama, laughter of the everyday scene. A feature is sort of like a sandwich, with slabs of frosted cake on each side and meat and potatoes, garnished with plenty of seasoning, in the middle.

How to Spot a Feature

Journalism students, assigned for the first time to find and write a feature story, occasionally return with a perplexed look and blank copy paper. The fault may lie with the instructor, who has failed to explain properly how to spot a feature story—how to recognize immediately the ingredients that lend themselves to feature treatment.

The widely known story about "Good Ol' Mel Miller of Peoria,

Ill.," serves as an example of how a professional writer can identify and handle a feature story that the amateur might ignore. Pat McNulty of the Associated Press visited in 1960 the Sandpiper Bar at the Marine Corps base in Laguna Beach, California. He heard the Marines talking about Good Ol' Mel in Peoria and, after asking a few questions, was told about a Mel Miller Vacation Fund— coins put into a 120-millimeter shell in the bar.

The Marines explained to McNulty that a Capt. Joe Gestson, who placed a long-distance call in quest of a lost automobile, inadvertently had reached a Melvin Miller of Peoria. He started a conversation with Miller anyway, and the acquaintance subsequently ripened through correspondence.

Miller had expressed an interest in visiting California, so the Marines started the fund to finance such a trip.

That was the situation when McNulty arrived on the scene. But he didn't write a word, hoping to keep the yarn exclusive until Miller got to the Marine Corps base for a VIP reception.

Then the Marines started selling Melvin Miller T-shirts and Melvin Miller pennants, and McNulty knew he couldn't keep the story a secret much longer. Meanwhile, the Chicago AP bureau phoned Miller and arranged for photographs before he left Peoria. When McNulty's first story moved on the wire, Wirephoto pictures were sent from Chicago.

Many newspapers played the story on front pages with multicolumn headlines and two or three photographs. Compliments rolled in quickly. The Akron *Beacon Journal* called the story "a real Saturday brightener." The Canton *Repository* labeled it "a superlative feature."

When Miller arrived in California, there were parades, a key to the city, a horse race named for him, a Hollywood tour and kisses from movie starlets, a visit to a bullfight, a Marine review, a bigleague ball game at which he threw out the first ball, a television appearance, and an unscheduled reunion with his wife.

Some newspapers wrote editorials about the whole delightful mishmash. The Des Moines *Tribune* commented on the "patience, humor, and generosity" of the principals. Other newspapers wrote features inspired by the Miller affair. The Dayton *Daily News*, for example, found Dayton's Mel Miller and reported his views in a page one story. And editors wrote letters. The telegraph editor of the Lafayette *Journal*, for instance, said: "There is a wide circle of McNulty admirers here waiting patiently for the next yarn by him. This McNulty is good."

Why did the story attract so much attention? Hub Keavy, Chief of the AP bureau at Los Angeles, gave one answer in a talk in San Francisco, saying:

> The Marines didn't make the story and Good Ol' Mel didn't either. It was made by a feature writer with imagination—Pat McNulty. His deft handling of a wacky situation created the new image for the average man—the new name for John Q. Public. Melvin Miller has become the symbol for the average American —and not necessarily from Peoria, either. As Capt. Gestson, now quite philosophical about it all, puts it, "There are millions of Melvin Millers all over the country."

McNulty's achievement, then, was twofold: he had the ability to recognize a feature story of national proportions and he had the talent to write it skillfully.

In 1961 professional newsmen saw readily the feature implications of a story with international appeal. Lyndon Johnson, then Vice-President, visited Pakistan and invited a humble camel driver, Bashir Ahmad, to visit the United States. Ahmad accepted the invitation, and the outpouring of feature material began long before he left his native country.

The AP resident correspondent in Karachi, Zamir Siddiqi, had a keen eye for the small, human details in the lives of his fellow men. One of his first features about Ahmad told of his preparations to visit America. As the *AP Log* later noted, "It became a story of all men, anywhere, who had ever left home and family behind for a trip to some exotic place—be it Paris, Atlantic City, or a trout stream fifty miles away." The story began:

Bashir Ahmad had sworn on the Koran before his wife and four children that he would not look at another woman during his visit to the United States.

Siddiqi told frankly how Ahmad had become the object of jealousy among his neighbors and the suspicions of his wife who feared he would marry a white woman. His relatives, said the story, were afraid he would eat pork and ham and drink liquor—all forbidden by his Moslem religion.

The feature gave the reader the impression he actually was conversing with the camel driver—a mark of good reporting and writing.

At about the time Bashir Ahmad became feature copy, a bit actor in Hollywood filed a property claim that tweaked the imagination of feature writers throughout Southern California. Pat Hawley, who said he had pored over old records, announced that no one ever had claimed the land on which the city of Laguna Beach had arisen. So he formally filed the appropriate papers in his own name.

His effort, of course, was doomed from the start, for city officials die hard and give up land even harder. But the incident made sparkling feature copy because an average guy had shaken up an entire city.

Hawley said later he didn't really want to take the whole city—only three thousand yards of expensive beachfront property.

"I'll put a fence around it," he told reporters.

What guideline can the beginning journalist infer from those examples? Merely that unusual events often lend themselves to feature treatment, whether they involve a mixed-up telephone call, a camel driver or a young man who fights city hall in a different way. The trick is to recognize the distinctive character of the event.

Asking Questions

Once a writer spots a potential feature story, he works as a reporter, asking questions and gathering facts. Rarely can he produce an effective feature without numerous queries, perhaps even extended inverviews.

In Seattle, a reporter drove to work for three years past a garage with two airplane pontoons on the roof. He often wondered why the pontoons were there and who owned them, but he never asked. The answers eventually appeared in the opposition newspaper, whose reporter had seen the pontoons and had asked a simple question: "Why are those pontoons on top of the garage?" The query, made on the front porch, led to a cup of coffee and an interview with the owner—an Alaska bush pilot who was delighted to describe flying experiences crammed with drama.

When President Kennedy's use of a rocking chair boosted that piece of furniture's popularity across the nation, one newsman started asking questions to determine the impact on firms that produced the rockers. He found, for instance, that the P & P Chair Co. in Asheboro, North Carolina, was so flooded with orders that a depression was ended in that area for several months. It was learned the President's use of the rocker, linked with his personal physician's endorsement of "rocking," had prompted the deluge of orders.

A *New York Times* reporter, Gay Talese, asked a simple question that led to a bright feature about the World War II Norden bombsight used in U.S. bombers. How much was one of the nation's top secret weapons in the 1940s worth today? The answer: $24.50, compared with a previous value of $25,000.

Wire service features occasionally are prompted by newspaper editors who ask questions, knowing that the AP or UPI can obtain information from their bureaus around the world. John McCormally, executive editor of the Hutchinson (Kansas) *News*, once asked the AP what Charles Lindbergh was doing thirty-five years after his historic flight to Paris. The AP demurred, primarily because of the belief Lindbergh would not talk to reporters, would not answer phone calls, and ignored letters. But McCormally persisted, maintaining even a negative story about his passion for privacy would be worthwhile. The result was a feature used in newspaper across the nation. It pointed out that Lindbergh wasn't a recluse as believed by many but was leading an active life.

Frequently one event with feature implications will suggest several questions, each the basis for a separate story. When topless swimsuits for women made their debut, secondary feature possibilities were many and varied. Were the suits lawful? What was the reaction of department store executives? What were the views of municipal officials? What were the opinions of film beauties? What were the thoughts of women who wore them?

In short, the writer-reporter must ask questions and more questions after he has recognized the feature characteristics of an event.

Starting the Feature

Paul O'Neil, a talented, veteran writer for *Life* magazine, has devised what he terms O'Neil's Law:

> Always grab the reader by the throat in the first paragraph, sink your thumbs into his windpipe in the second, and hold him against the wall until the tag line.

The law is especially applicable to feature writers, for most feature stories are transitory and unessential. Readers should be told who won the race for mayor or what is happening in a murder case, but they can get along rather well without knowing how much a Norden bombsight costs today or whether Melvin Miller has arrived in California. Consequently, the feature starts behind the proverbial eight ball. As mere frosting on the cake it must attract the reader, then hold his interest. The feature writer must inject some punch, some dash into the lead or opening of the story. Several methods are used effectively to achieve such a beginning. Among them are these:

Contrast. The reader's attention can be gained if he immediately is told about some unlikely, unexpected event or situation, or is told that something he is accustomed to has changed:

> BOURNEMOUTH, England (AP)—One of Britain's biggest nudist clubs today denounced topless dresses and bathing suits as indecent.

> BEVERLY HILLS, Calif. (AP)—A bandit paused during a $100,000 robbery today to give the victim a heart pill. Police said the pill may have saved Herbert Kronish's life.

> PORTLAND, Maine (UPI)—In this age of nuclear power, the oldest privately supported welfare society of its kind in the nation is still providing firewood to warm the homes of needy widows.

> WASHINGTON (UPI)—The "war on poverty" may find out in 1966 how it feels to be poor. (Because of rising costs of war in Viet Nam)

Suspended interest. This approach, which somewhat resembles the beginning of a short story, piques the reader's curiosity by forcing him to wonder what comes next. Consequently, he continues with the story if the first sentences have aroused certain questions. He may find the answer in the second sentence or the tenth or even the final sentence. An example:

> BURBANK, Calif. (AP)—A quiet, graying man walked into the employment office of the huge Lockheed Aircraft Corp. plant and asked for a job.
> He filled out a routine form, turned it in, and went home to wait for an answer.
> Inside the plant, the form caused a furor.

An employment executive glanced through it and grabbed for a phone.

"Hey, we got some kind of a nut here who says he knows you," the man told Hall L. Hibbard, Senior Vice-President. "He says he also knows just about everybody on the board of directors.

"And get this, where the application asks about previous employment at Lockheed, the guy writes down: 'President.'"

"That's no nut," Hibbard said. "That can't be anyone but Lloyd Stearman."

He was right.

Characteristically, Lloyd Stearman, one of the greats of aviation and first President of Lockheed Aircraft Corp. when it was formed from a bankrupt firm in 1932, sought no help from any of his old friends when he decided he wanted to design airplanes again.

All of the above may properly be termed the lead for that feature story. The technique appears simple; actually, it involves immediate identification with the reader (a man seeking employment), an immediate question (Why is a graying man looking for a job?), a secondary question (Why did the application cause a furor?), lively quotation ("Hey, we got some kind of a nut here"), and another question (Was he really a former president of the firm?). Then it suggests one more question to lead the reader into the body of the story—why would a former president of the company apply years later for a job at the same firm? The format is intended to tempt the reader, to make him want to proceed with the story.

The same style can be used for a shorter story:

LONDON (AP)—Bookmaker Peter Mortimer advertised his car for sale for 450 pounds ($1,260) and added that he was prepared to toss a coin for double or nothing.

Auto dealer William Costello took him up on it Saturday and tossed the coin. Mortimer called heads. The coin came down tails. Costello drove away with a free auto.

Having read the first sentence of that story, the reader naturally asks, "Did he win or lose?" So he keeps reading to find out.

Another example:

UNITED PRESS INTERNATIONAL—Mrs. Marion West Higgins, the Republican lady from Bergen County, had the floor in the assembly of the State of New Jersey.

She spoke of how proud she was to be the first woman ever elected Speaker of the New Jersey assembly. She talked about her record and of how it felt to be a political loser. Then she stopped and the legislature adjourned.

It was a rainy day last December—and a half century of Republican rule had just come to an end in the legislature of the Garden State.

For the first time since President-elect Thomas Woodrow Wilson sat in the New Jersey governor's chair fifty-three years ago, Democrats coming into office this month were wholly in control of the state legislature.

The reason could be summed up in one word: reapportionment.

A similar example:

LOS ANGELES (AP)—He never buttons his ministerial robe. Sometimes he leans an elbow on the pulpit.

If another speaker bores him, he silently translates the dull monologue into Italian, Spanish, or French—or surreptitiously studies population figures from a pocket calendar—to keep himself awake.

Next year Rabbi Edgar F. Magnin will complete fifty years with the same congregation, one of the biggest and wealthiest of his faith.

Quotation. Though regarded by some editors and journalism instructors as a cowardly way to begin a newspaper story, the quote lead can be employed effectively in a feature article. The test, of course, is whether the quotation will prompt the reader to continue. Here are examples:

PHILADELPHIA (AP)—"Quick," said the man, as he hopped into a cab, "get me out of here—the police are after me."

"They're not only after you, they've got you," said the driver, Highway Patrolman George Sternberger, who was posing as a cabbie to try to halt cab holdups.

RIO DE JANEIRO (UPI)—"There goes Violet's tool shed," my wife said as a cracking sound, followed by a roar and splintering of wood, came from across the street. Another larger roar followed.

"That must be the stone retaining wall of Alexandrino Street," she said.

She was right each time.

That's the way it was Tuesday night, all night on Santa Teresa Hill, in the worst recorded rainstorm in the city's history.

Play on words. One of the most common beginnings for a feature story is a different version of a widely known expression or a sequence of words that lends itself to humor:

HOLLYWOOD (AP)—Steven Hill launched his acting career by putting his worst foot forward—and the other in his mouth.

RICHMOND, Va. (UPI)—Beadle Bumble, a character in the novel *Oliver Twist* by Charles Dickens, was a stupid public official.

The Richmond *News Leader's* "Beadle Bumble Fund," used for the "sole object of redressing the stupidities of the public officials," is growing fat.

The newspaper's condemnation of the action of the Hanover County School Board in banning the novel *To Kill a Mockingbird* prompted donations to the fund totaling more than $80.

SALMON, Idaho (AP)—There was a moose loose behind the Dodge Garage in this town early Thursday.

LEOMINSTER, Mass. (UPI)—The government will salute this year a canny Yankee who realized that apples were the fruit if not the spice of frontier life.

NEW YORK (AP)—Depending on how the law's construed, there's nothing rude about a proper nude as long as her mood skirts the lewd.

Factual. Often the beginning of a feature story needs no embellishment. The writer simply lets the facts tell the story. An example:

COMPTON, Calif. (AP)—Daniel Elmore, 72, a Negro handyman, was graduated from high school Wednesday.

He is a little late getting his diploma because he had to put all ten of his sons and daughters through college first.

Animals need not be glamorized to arouse interest:

> WESTERLY, R.I. (UPI)—Pets have joined the international
> jet set.
> Animal globe-hopping has made giraffelike strides in recent
> years, according to Bed Rock Dogs International, a kind of travel
> agency for pets.
> In 1965, Bed Rock made travel arrangements for more than
> seven hundred animals, six times as many as eight years ago, when
> it began operation, and 30 per cent above the 1964 total.

There are other possible beginnings for feature stories—many
others. The primary question that should be asked for each beginning is, "Does it gain the reader's attention and lead him into the
story?" If it does, the lead probably is appropriate.

Some Complete Stories

The student of journalism should examine closely feature stories
by professionals, studying structure, style, choice of words, and
ending. Here are two by Douglass Welch of the Seattle *Post-
Intelligencer,* both examples of how to present a single idea in an
original form that maintains reader interest:

> Schell Creek at Edmonds went green the other day.
> It was not just a little bit green. It was very green.
> Usually, it is a dirty brown.
> "What happened to our pretty dirty brown river?" people asked
> one another.
> Police Chief Ruben Grimstad volunteered to find out.
> He conceived it to be his duty.
> He puts duty above all else.
> He started up the river.
> He was whistling, "Up the lonely river . . ."
> "There goes our Chief on his appointed rounds," people said.
> "We can sleep safely tonight."

The Chief hadn't walked very far until he found the creek a familiar dirty brown again.

"This is very strange," he mused. "Above this point our little creek is dirty brown. Below this point it is a brilliant green."

Clearly, the situation called for thinking through.

The Chief thought through.

"There must be something at this point," he reasoned, "that causes the creek to change from a dirty brown to a brilliant green."

It is thinking like this that made America great.

Come to find out, a couple of small boys had thrown some Air Force life raft marker dye in the water.

Where on earth did they get it? you ask breathlessly.

They got it out of a war surplus raft which the father of one of them had purchased.

They had wondered if the dye would work.

Don't call it idle juvenile curiosity. Call it the Spirit of Higher Experimentation. Experimentation made America great, too.

But the Chief made Schell Creek a pretty dirty brown again.

He confiscated the dye.

Anything can happen at Edmonds.

Q—You are Mr. W. J. Billings, division manager for Western Washington for the Pacific Telephone and Telegraph Company.

A—Yes, I am.

Q—And I believe you have something you want to tell the readers of the *Post-Intelligencer* this morning?

A—Yes, I wanted to tell them that we are building here in Seattle the world's largest No. 5 crossbar office.

Q—How's that again?

A—The world's largest No. 5 crossbar office.

Q—What is a No. 5 crossbar office?

A—That's a telephone term for the largest type of automatic switching equipment which does so many amazing things. It has a magic brain and all that.

Q—Where is it located?

A—At our new building at 1122–3rd Ave. We hope to have it operating by 1958. By that time we will have spent five years and $13 million dollars.

Q—That's a lot of dough.

A—Yes, it is, and for it we are getting the largest telephone exchange of its type in the whole world. It will permit customers in the Main, Elliott, and Seneca exchanges to dial direct over long

distances. And it will keep count of what they are doing, who's
doing it, and how long it is being done, and like that.

Q—Do you have some statistics for us?

A—Yes, I have. More than 280 Western Electric installers are at
work. They are using 5,000 blueprints, in a stack 60 feet high, to
find the spots where they will melt 900 pounds of solder. They are
using 350 soldering irons. There will be 2,500,000 connections.

Q—Those Western Electric people certainly have connections.

A—Please. The 280 installers are using 400 screwdrivers, 600
pairs of diagonals, and heaven only knows how many long noses.

Q—Long noses?

A—That's a type of plier. Forty-four huge cables carry 37,500
pairs of wires through a tunnel 15 feet under Seneca St. between
the main telephone building and the 1122–3d Ave. building. The
splicers are splicing these and another 57,000 together. A total of
94,500 pairs of wires will be spliced before this job is complete.

Q—That's a lot of splicing.

A—Indeed, it is. The first really permanent residents of the new
building are two groups of operators. The centralized information
bureau moved in early in January and the Unit No. 1 long distance
operators followed them through the Seneca St. tunnel a month
later.

Q—Did the long distance girls actually walk through the tunnel?

A—Yes, they did.

Q—You're pretty proud of this new installation, hey, Mr. Billings?

A—I think it is the gosh-darndest collection of ultramodern
switching I've ever seen.

Q—Please, Mr. Billings, let's watch the language. Let's not be
carried away.

A—Think of it! Nine hundred and fifty-two frames of No. 5
crossbar equipment bolted down on three floors! Imagine!

Q—I know, I know. Please, Mr. Billings.

A—It leaves me kind of breathless. Do you know that about 150
million conductor-feet of wire winds through the building? That's
enough to run a 30-pin, open-wire lead between Los Angeles and
Seattle.

Q—Let's leave Los Angeles out of this.

A—I want to show you a picture of one of our installers at work.
Look at all the wires!

Q—What do you call a mess of wires like that? Do you call them spaghetti or something?

A—No, we just call them wires. That's John Halvorsen in the picture. He's been working steadily since June 1956.

Q—And you say when he's not working, he's hunting for needles in haystacks at home, for laughs?

A—I didn't say that. You said that. I want to say something about the building. It is 111 feet by 130 feet and six stories high with basement. We think it is earthquake proof and atomic bomb resistant. We won't know exactly until someone sets a bomb off.

Inevitably, some students and editors will criticize the length of this story—and with considerable justification. But it does make out-of-the-ordinary copy for a day when there is room in the paper for a tongue-in-cheek or whimsical story.

In contrast to Welch's stories is this feature by Dial Torgerson of the Associated Press:

SAN DIEGO, Calif. (AP)—A blind boy stood by the helicopter, waiting for President Kennedy.

"I'm Fred Korth," said a tall man with a gentle voice. "I'm the Secretary of the Navy."

"How do you do, Mr. Korth," said Joey Renzi, age 11. "Is he coming? Is the President coming?"

"No, not yet," said Korth. "Don't worry. We won't let him get away without seeing you. He wants to meet you."

It was a letter in Braille that Joey wrote to Kennedy which attracted the President's attention. In it Joey told how he wanted to shake the President's hand because "it wouldn't do me any good to stand on the roadside while all the other kids are watching."

That's how it was that a blind boy was waiting at the Marine Corps recruit depot with the high-ranking officials alongside the helicopter which was to take Kennedy away to an aircraft carrier at sea.

The boy—born prematurely—has been blind virtually all his life. Doctors say an over-rich oxygen mixture in an incubator caused hemorrhages which destroyed his sight.

But he can see a great deal with his hands as he did Thursday when, in his mind's own bright pictures, he saw the President.

All Joey heard was a big car stop. He felt a large hand reach for and another touch his shoulder.

He told afterward what was said:

"He said he enjoyed seeing me, and I told him what an honor it was to meet him, and he gave me a tie clasp, and I gave him my letter. And he said, 'I hope you can come to the White House and visit me sometime.'"

The tie clasp was a gold miniature PT boat with the name "Kennedy" on it.

The boy's letter told the President, "I will treasure this experience all my life."

What could Joey's hands tell him about the President?

"He's kind of tall," said Joey. "He's real neat looking. He has kind of like an English—no, I guess it's a New England—accent. And he has a strong grip. A real strong grip for a big, important man like the President."

After their brief talk, the President climbed into the waiting helicopter, the engine roared, and dust flew.

"Good-bye, Mr. Kennedy," Joey shouted into the wind blast. "Good-bye, sir!"

"Can he see me?" he asked. "Did he wave back?"

"Yes," Joey was told, "he waved."

Joey listened as the helicopter flew out of sight.

"This has been the best day of my life—ever," he said.

Features exist everywhere, just waiting to be identified and written. Too often we pass them by as impractical or unobtainable. The best rule is, try it. The result may surprise you. Remember, once upon a time a feature writer wondered what it would be like to ride in one of the Brink's Inc. armored trucks. He was told that no outsider had ridden in one of its vehicles in the firm's 106 years. But he asked anyway.

The answer was "Yes."

IX

Newspaper, News Service, Radio-TV News Writing — How They Differ

If the preceding chapters have been read with care, it should be obvious to the student at this point that *sentence structure* is the foundation of news writing in all its forms—newspapers, wire services, radio, and television. There are, however, distinctive differences in the processing of sentences for these primary media.

The important ones are variations in *point of view*. The writer must know the nature of his audience and his relationship to it before he can compose his story.

As a common denominator, the sentence is *printed* in the first two cases, *spoken* in the others. Whatever the means of delivery, *sentences* must be written at the outset. They will not, however, be cast in precisely the same way. *Content* and *emphasis* of the sentence will vary according to the medium because each audience calls for special treatment.

The newspaper reporter is concerned chiefly with the local

scene. The wire service writer sets his sights upon readers beyond the city, beyond the state, often beyond the nation. The fields of radio and television newsmen also may extend beyond city and state. But they serve audiences that are *listening*, not *reading*.

The television newscaster, of course, is additionally concerned with an audience that *sees*. The spoken word, the expressions of the announcer, the use of still photos or motion pictures, and sometimes on-the-spot visual reports—all are transmitted to the TV receiver.

Newspapers own radio and TV stations. Wire services prepare special reports for radio and TV newsrooms and deliver them by a network of special circuits. Larger radio and television stations commonly utilize the wire service reports prepared primarily for newspapers, in addition to the radio-TV wires. This linkage of all four media makes it possible for a journalism graduate to progress from one to another in sequence if he so desires. He would have to make a series of adjustments to function seccessfully under dissimilar circumstances.

The Newspaper Pattern

Consider first the conditions a new graduate would face in his first job—on a daily afternoon paper in a county seat city of 120,000. The standard of writing is high, the staff is large enough to provide considerable individual competition for advancement, and the diversity of news sources, including government agencies, is sufficient to offer wide experience. Afternoon papers must be produced more rapidly than morning papers, so a good test of speed and skill is available.

A typical sequence of performances over a five- to seven-year period would include: suburban correspondence, general assignment reporting, copydesk work, specialized editing (telegraph desk, city desk, sports, etc.).

Correspondence. Assignment to a hinterland bureau calls for the expectable amount of secondary news customarily found in suburban editions. It also necessitates a certain degree of self-reliance in handling major news breaks because advice and help from the city room are not readily available. Hours are likely to be irregular; the big traffic accidents, for instance, have a tendency to occur at awkward times of the night. And the copy of a suburban reporter can undergo a discouraging degree of revision upon reaching the city room. Much of the work is dull. In writing for the suburban edition a correspondent probably will include more detail, just as he will emphasize local names. Such editions are intended to replace, or compete with, small local papers.

Beat man. After six to eight months in Suburbia, assignment to the county courthouse in the city distinctly broadens the horizon. It may also produce, initially, moments of apprehension. Covering a criminal trial in actual fact is not quite the same as reporting a fictitious case devised by a journalism instructor for next day's class. There are very real hazards of misquotation and libel in recounting courtroom utterances and procedures. Knowledge of basic legal practices is assumed by most city desks to be part of a reporter's qualification.

If a defendant or a key witness in the criminal action comes from an outlying town, the reporter must satisfy not only the early city editions but the suburban edition and the home-delivered final as well, updating his story as developments take place. This affects the content of his stories written for one audience or the other. Some details pertinent to suburban readers would be omitted from the version for city editions, and vice versa.

The beat man who successfully negotiates such hurdles has taken the first step toward professionalism; he is on his way to becoming a specialist of sorts. For the careful reporter, daily contact with members of the board of supervisors and other officials is rewarding. He can earn their trust and become privy to confidential information which will enable him to anticipate news before it becomes publishable.

This growing intimacy with people and procedures within officialdom also will enhance the reporter's self-assurance. Simultaneously, these gains will increase the respect with which the city desk regards his developing knowledge of public affairs.

The desk probably will encourage him to tackle special projects of in-depth reporting. His growing background will make possible advance and follow-up pieces on important programs or decisions of various commissions and departments, or stories interpreting the results of official actions.

General assignment.   Good beat men often keep their posts for years. But just as often the reporter on his first paper is deemed in need of exposure to other activities, if his full worth is to evolve. At this point transfer to the general assignment staff is expectable.

Here the variety of subject matter is much broader. The field embraces everything from features to the unanticipated fast-breaking story—a tornado, a commercial airline accident, a sensational murder.

General assignment men learn to work in crews on occasion. They also learn to be ready for anything. This calls for a good basic knowledge of many things and many prominent people. When the story breaks it is not always possible to bone up in the library before leaving the office.

The rewrite battery.   When several general assignment reporters—and possibly a beat man as well—are dispatched on a hot story, the desk frequently divides the angles of coverage. Those assigned may not even be located close to one another. In a manhunt or a kidnaping, for example, one or more may be in the field, another at headquarters, another at the home of the victim.

In such a case their independent phone-ins are handled by the rewrite man, who weaves their contributions into a colorful, comprehensive whole.

One asset successful rewrite men and general assignment reporters have in common is versatility. Each must possess a wide informational background. Either might handle an agricultural story at one hour and a medical convention thirty minutes thereafter. In many cases the rewrite man may be more skillful in phrasing than the reporter in the field, but on the other hand the general assignment reporter may be the better legman. Some reporters have that rare ability to ferret out news under difficult circumstances, yet their written account may not be superior. The rewrite man, working in the office, knows his editor's needs in length and in organization of a story, whereas the reporter under the influence of the scene may fall prey to wordiness and minor detail. The rewrite man also knows the questions to ask the reporter to insure a clear and well-rounded story.

Then, too, there is a physical factor to consider: the finest writer may be the poorest man to send to a riot or a train wreck. He might not be able to run fast enough to save his neck or to garner a telephone. Scores of city rooms have a fair share of fat—and first-rate—rewrite men, or men whose age is a handicap on the breaking news front. Many rewrite men are so perceptive in envisioning a scene or situation that they can make a highly impressive story out of routine phoned-in notes. On the whole, however, the rewrite man and the general assignment man work as a team, and many newspapers grant them joint bylines.

On some dailies the general assignment staff is also the rewrite battery, in whole or at least in part. When there is no story of major proportions to take him out of the office, or not enough such stories to take all of the manpower into the field, the general assignment reporter functions as a rewrite man developing stories by phone in the office, taking material from those who are out on assignments, handling the calls of beat men making a deadline, or receiving the contributions of suburban stringers and ordinary readers with a story to volunteer.

Copydesk. It is legendary that, in the eyes of the front office, the best way a managing editor can justify a raise for an outstanding writer is to move him to the copydesk. This type of promotion is patently anomalous. Having acquired, or trained, an exceptional phrasemaker the editor by such action has rewarded him by putting him where he can't write anything but headlines. Furthermore, it is well known in the business that most of the best writers make the poorest editors. There are exceptions, of course. But good editors, like good writers, are trained. Those who show special aptitude, in either area, are the easiest and quickest to break in. Among journalism students the presence of this aptitude should become apparent considerably before graduation, and many times a man in his first job will know in which direction he will go. The potential editor may be assigned first to reporting, to give him the "feel" of the paper and the awareness of practicing professionally those things he has been taught in the classroom. But the managing editor in such cases probably has decided already that in six months or a year he will put this particular neophyte on the copydesk.

Reporters must know the language in which they undertake to write, but copy editors must know it even more completely. They must be experts in the choice of the right word, in the structure of the correct, simple, clear sentence that says exactly what it was intended to say. In short, they must make certain that the reporter has avoided the pitfalls this book has covered in delineating the quality of writing upon which true communication is based.

This means a knowledge of grammar and syntax. It means a sensitivity to appropriate, tasteful phrasing. It means a feeling for clarity, euphony, and organization. It means that all of the factors cited earlier as related to the writer also apply equally to the editor.

Desk men have other responsibilities. Perhaps the gravest of these is to make certain of factual accuracy. It is one thing to change a word the reporter has used injudiciously; it is definitely another to change the meaning of a sentence written by the man at the scene. If he has any reason to suspect that the writer did not say exactly what he meant to say, it is the role of the copy editor to check back with the reporter, or ask the city desk to do so. If the reporter's own knowledge is at fault—as in a geographical error—the copy reader must be smart enough to detect this. Good deskmen have a special talent for "smelling" something wrong. Perhaps they know what it is, perhaps they don't. But they know how to use the library.

Deskmen also have to know how to meet space limitations by reducing a story without committing mayhem. This is an art in itself. Does the end product contain all that is significant in the reporter's account? If it does not, the editor has cut too deeply, or the writer has been remiss in the first place.

Another copydesk virtue is a consciousness of form. Is the story properly organized, or should some of its paragraphs be switched? Is the most important part of the information embodied in the lead, or is it buried two hundred words down? Is the continuity proper, or should the piece be handed back to a rewrite man?

Copy editors write headlines. Some are good at it; some are better at copy editing; some are good at both. Good headlines *fit*—not only the type count prescribed but the content of the story as well. Among the headlines we see too often is the one based on some angle deep in the story. This may or may not be the wrong headline. But one thing is certain: either the head or the story is wrong in emphasis.

Writing headlines is a very particularized chore, about which it is difficult to offer concrete guidance. Apart from the requirement that headline and story shall conform, most of the rules are mechanical, in that they apply to matters of typography and editorial policy.

True, letter count is not so restricted as it was in the days when the balanced head was almost universal. A few venerable publications—*The New York Times* is one—still adhere stubbornly to the uniform unit count for each line of the main banks, but the step-head is the accepted form today on most papers large and small. This can be written faster, and the latitude it allows undoubtedly makes easier the production of a headline that more accurately reflects the main message of the story. Few will argue that the time required in forging a perfectly balanced headline is worthwhile if the result does not faithfully follow the facts of the news. With the rigid unit count this was sometimes impossible to achieve.

But the principal reason why it is hard to help the novice head-line writer is that every paper has its preferred type sizes for head-lines, nearly all of them varying widely in unit count. That is why —as has been mentioned in earlier pages—attempts to teach headline writing in college are largely a waste of time and effort that could be devoted to basic writing or to other aspects of jour-nalistic training. For the deskman, moving from one paper to an-other is very much like starting over again.

Furthermore, whether headlines are balanced or stepped, the matter of policy is still with us. Here again there is great disparity among newspapers. Some permit prepositions at the end of a line. Some don't. Some insist that each line shall comprise a complete thought or idea. Some ban the headline starting with a verb form. Some sanction headlines without any verbs at all. You learn what's wanted, and how to do it, after you're hired. No school of journalism can be expected to anticipate the answer to this prob-lem.

A copyreader's routine is largely peaks and valleys—furious effort just before deadlines, semi-idleness between editions. None-theless, this way of work is the breath of life to some. Very likely they will become telegraph editors, city editors, or news editors. As such their general knowledge and judgment will determine which stories will be chosen and what places they will occupy in the paper.

But for others the copydesk will prove to be nothing more than the aforementioned opportunity for a modest raise in pay. Sitting all day long, time passes slowly. The chances are a copy boy sharpens their pencils and keeps the coffee cups filled. These are the copyreaders who chop up paper endlessly when they aren't busy. They're bored because they really belong on the reportorial staff. Good writers should write. But not many will go back to the domain of the city desk. This might be regarded as a loss of status in the eyes of management.

Most of them adjust finally to the conditions that prevail around the rim. There, happy or unhappy, they wait for promotion to departmental editorships—or for retirement.

The News Services

Deskmen who are rewarded writers are welcomed by news services. Experience in copy editing is not a prerequisite, but it is a recommendation. This does not mean that the good writer without desk experience will be shunned. But, once hired, he soon will realize that multiple duties are characteristic of AP and UPI jobs. Ultimately all staffers are expected to be able to function in either capacity—writer or editor—if necessary.

Scope is perhaps the first factor that impresses those who make the switch to a news agency. As newspaper reporters they were chiefly concerned with the local scene. But now the writer's audience may involve the whole world, and his point of view must be realigned commensurately. He will continue to write about local happenings, but the events he reports will be those significant to readers *outside* his city. These will comprise the cream of the day's occurrences.

His new obligations will be gratifyingly free of trivia. The hard news and the most widely interesting feature material will command his time and effort. Although he will not be burdened by the inconsequential, he will have to supply a certain amount of background to make his account meaningful in other cities, states, and countries. Some of this will be reader information which a newspaper can take for granted in its largely localized audience. An example would be the geographic nature of the community.

To meet their particular needs, AP and UPI maintain a variety of side circuits, including message wires, interbureau collection wires, sports wires, market wires. But, in each service there are two principal circuits—the "A" wire and the "B" wire. The "A" spans the nation and carries the top news in all directions. Its stories are those practically all papers will print, in whole or in part. By this route the report of a major earthquake in California will be delivered throughout the country and, from New York, will be relayed overseas. By the same facility, in reverse, papers across the nation will receive word of a revolution in Greece. New York is the control point for the "A" wire.

The "B" is a regional wire for news significant or interesting to a more limited degree, or to a more limited geographic area. For example, the AP's "B" wire serves the states from New York westward. A California story of prime concern to the mining industry, or the livestock business, would not normally be filed on the "A" (unless something cataclysmic has happened) because vast areas of the nation and the world are not very interested. But the story is a natural for the "B" since it will be widely printed in the West. Scattered areas in foreign lands where cattle and mining are vital activities also will get it, through relays.

Kansas City or Chicago is not the end of the "B" line. The states eastward have their own counterparts for regional news, and the New York control editors relay from one to another, in either direction. An example would be a survey story about the southern California citrus industry, not high enough in general news value to warrant transmission throughout the country on the "A." Arizona papers will want it; Texas will want it. But Florida also will want it, and New York will relay it on the regional circuit which serves the southeastern states.

The "B" is also valuable for moving one-pointers. These are stories of interest in one, or perhaps two, specific locales. Examples are legion, among them stories involving arrests or auto accident victims who reside in another state. Because the rest of the nation has no interest in this particular accident or arrest, use of the "B" avoids cluttering the prime, transcontinental "A" wire.

The purposes and operation of the various wires, together with many other peculiarities of news service operation, really are not more complicated than the techniques of producing a sizable city daily. But they are unique, and inevitably they will bewilder the newcomer for a time, however many years he may have spent working for newspapers. Strangely enough, one day they will fall into their proper places in his mind, because they do indeed follow a very specific pattern.

When this happens the novice wire service staffer will realize just how much his new worldwide point of view depends upon *judgment*—judgment by the writer in determining which facts belong in his story and which details he should leave out and judgment by the editor in deciding how long each story should be and where among his many wires he should file it. On newspapers the burden of judgment is more widely shared.

Resourcefulness is another necessity. With few exceptions wire service bureaus are by no means so generously manned as are metropolitan newspapers, yet they may be called upon to provide coverage of any magnitude. If disaster strikes—such as racial strife on the scale of the 1965 Watts riots in Los Angeles, the local bureau staff may be augmented by a dozen men or more from other bureaus, including New York. But even the chores of a "normal" day may tax the ingenuity and the energy of the local bureau. Except in Washington, New York and some foreign capitals, news services have few if any beat men. On newspapers beat men have daily contact with news sources. Wire services rarely enjoy this sort of professional intimacy, again with the mentioned exceptions; for them, information sometimes is hard to come by, particularly at night. This is why AP and UPI staffers become specialists in functioning by phone.

There are some compensations for limited staffs. One advantage held by AP alone is access to carbon copies of every story produced by its member papers in every city where the news agency maintains offices. This boon extends also to pre-publication perusal by stringers of copy written for member papers in surrounding cities. These papers are numerous; in some cases two states comprise the area for which one bureau is responsible.

Advance access to members' stories is part of the agreement between the newspapers and the AP. A cooperative, the AP relates to these papers on the standard of mutual news exchange. The expense of AP coverage everywhere in the world is prorated among its members on a nonprofit basis. The United Press International, a privately owned profit-making organization, lacks the privilege of seeing before publication the carbons of stories written for papers that buy the service. In bureau cities UPI must wait until local dailies are on the street. That is why, in most large cities, UPI is forced to cover in person more events than AP does.

In both services every bureau has the help of its neighboring bureaus. It works this way: One service has a good story out of Las Vegas, Nevada. The opposition wants to match it, but its Las Vegas correspondent hasn't been able to get it. The Los Angeles bureau thereupon appeals to Reno or asks the San Francisco bureau to do so. Reno may have the needed information or may be able to get it from sources unavailable to Las Vegas.

The same procedure is used in gathering special facts to enhance a story already in hand.

It has been said that working for a wire service is like working for three thousand employers. This is true to the extent that the member's wish is the staffer's command. When a paper in one state wants a special story in another state or another city, the news agency bureau nearest the event will go to exceptional lengths to get it. Sometimes this is easy; usually it entails problems. A member in the bureau's city, or nearby, may have the information or may send a reporter to get it. Otherwise the bureau's staff will dig it up, most often by phone. If this is impossible and the manpower is low on a given day, an off-duty man may be called in on overtime to do the job, provided the requesting member is willing to be assessed for the added expense. In any event, the relationship between the service and the member who buys it is as close as that in any commercial or fraternal operation you could name—and the results are much faster.

Most requests are made on the interbureau message wire. They range from feature stories and interpretives to incidental data someone needs for a roundup. Some seem silly or insignificant, involving details that would never reach any wire in the normal course, but the same conscientious effort to get them is demonstrated because a member *wants* them. His purpose, after all, may be an investigative story, which, when assembled, the wire service will be glad to pick up. If the wanted material runs to considerable length it will be sent to the member on a side circuit, or overhead by Western Union, or by mail. If time is the chief factor it may be phoned. Such telephonic requests from members as distant as New Zealand are frequent.

Policy.   Wire services hold themselves to be the epitome of neutrality. Some newspapers and broadcasters consider one service a better example of this than the other, but the truth is that neither could function without strife if it were biased in its viewpoint or its writing.

For reasons both ethical and practical, wire services do not editorialize. They deal in facts alone because this is the only honest (ethical) way to serve publications of every political and social shading. Any deviation from the facts is impractical because it will bring instant complaint from one or another segment of these publications.

Even an inadvertent semi-editorial phrasing in a single sentence has been known to arouse protests among members or clients. In fact, there have been cases in which a newspaper whose policy coincided with the accidentally slanted phrase has joined in the objection to it on the ground that editorial comment belongs on the editorial page and not in the news columns.

Controversial stories—those involving labor and politics are the most numerous—must be balanced in news service accounts.

Many times stories are withheld from the wire until the opposite side of the case can be presented. If it becomes evident that the facts on one side will not soon be available, the story so states. When these facts are obtained, they are immediately inserted.

It could be assumed from this neutral state that news services have no policy at all. But this would be true only to the point that they have no editorial or commercial preferences.

Such a climate is greatly valued by a vast number of news writers and, unquestionably, inspires many to shift from dailies to wire services.

Advertising, concededly a financial necessity of daily publications, at times exerts pressures that reporters and editors must learn to withstand. Certain newsmen, however, find that on some newspapers the appeasement of advertisers—by omission or commission—impedes their best performance.

Do they escape all such pressures by moving to news services? Yes and no. Yes, they avoid reprehensible influences to print what is not news or to censor that which is derogatory. No, they retain obligations to the money sources which indirectly pay their salaries, but the relationship is nonetheless honest, and it does not interfere with the truthful reporting of the news. No news service staffer is required or expected to provide an inaccurate or slanted story merely because a member paper asks for it. Neither will he deliver press agentry on request. News service writers and editors deal in facts alone, whether or not they are pleasing.

Some newspapers let opinion creep into the news columns. This does not always take the form of an editorialized sentence or paragraph; it may evidence itself as emphasis. For instance a publication that is inclined to be anti-union, in policy or in practice, may present both sides of a labor dispute, but its story will devote more space to management's position than it does to the union's complaints. Editorial policy also can be carried out by omission— the name of a big advertiser who becomes embroiled in the law may be left out, or the entire occurrence may be ignored. Not long ago a newspaper won a prize for riot coverage even though it did not send a single reporter to the scene on the first night of vio-lence. Racial bloodshed was not supposed to take place in this paper's fair city. Fortunately, the facts were faced in a day or two, and the paper fulfilled its obligation to the public with commend-able zeal.

Newspapers that slant the news will deny that anyone ever told a reporter what to put in his story. But the fact is that a newspa-per reporter of any intelligence above the moron does not have to be *told*. He has learned in short order what his publisher favors and disfavors. If he happens to be lacking in ethics, he will use his opportunities to follow the line his boss likes best. More often than not, this involves omission, and it could be called a form of automatic censorship.

Because wire service people must depend heavily upon news-papers it is imperative that they are ever alert to spot and delete slanting in every form. Omission of pertinent (embarrassing?) facts in a newspaper story necessitates special checking in the wire service bureau so that a balanced account can be written for the wire. Editorial coloration in a newspaper must be eliminated in the wire version in order to meet the needs of *all* those who buy the news service. Prime areas to watch for signs of favoritism are the newspaper reports of crime, politics, and labor.

Policy, then, in wire services is a matter of fairness and good taste. There are no sacred cows, no editorials, no tinted writing.

Adjusting.   Unlike newspapers, news services have a perpetual deadline. Whatever the hour, day or night, some newspapers, somewhere, need the top news *right now*. This suggests a condi-tion of constant speed. Yet the scene in an AP or UPI bureau is generally calmer than that of most newspaper city rooms at dead-line. The clattering, bell-ringing cacophony of teletypes is disturb-ing at first. It will always be heard, but, after a few weeks, not consciously. The newcomer must expect to be affected initially by the invisible state of urgency and the noise. He must also believe what he is told: that he will, definitely, get used to it.

Speed does evidence itself visibly when a bulletin story is developing, but this is not a chore for the recent arrival. Almost always veterans are utilized, at the typewriter and the desk, because handling a fast-breaking story of national or international import requires full knowledge of wire service procedure, a certain degree of experience, and complete adjustment to emergency conditions. Bulletin stories are not for those easily flustered, and overexcitement naturally is usual among beginners. Bulletin copy, from the lead onward, is ripped from the typewriter a few paragraphs at a time, to keep the story moving on the wire without a break if possible. If the writer is composing the piece in the office he must be able to organize as he goes and to type as fast as deskman and operator can edit and punch tape. If the man at the typewriter is taking the story by dictation from a staffer in the field, both of them must keep organization and phrasing constantly in mind. The editor who is filing the piece must make certain that they do so, changing the text or the order of filing the pieces if they fail.

It is a complicated, tense job all around. That is why, when possible, bureaus keep preparedness material on hand—chiefly for obituaries—so that, after the bulletin and the initial circumstances of the event have been laid down, the prepared copy can be fed steadily to the operator. The death of a movie star who has been ill long enough to permit the assembly of a preparedness story is a good example of the bulletin movement situation.

Those new to wire services are not likely to be exposed prematurely to this process, except in extreme emergency. They will be occupied with becoming acclimated. They will, for one thing, adjust to irregular hours—and these can vary amazingly within a 40-hour work week despite the best efforts to maintain normal schedules. Staffers may work two days and three nights, or any other combination, in a week. Show-up times, in day or night cycles, can be almost any hour. Some day tricks start at 5 or 6 A.M. Some overnight schedules begin at 1 A.M. or even 3 A.M.

This irregularity is part of the price paid for wire service employment, and the staffer must be willing to conform. If he isn't he had better stay with a newspaper, where his chances of avoiding the "lobster" trick are far better.

The same advice applies to those who join a wire service and then find their lives turned topsy-turvy by travel or transfer. Such is the nature of the business, and it is reasonable to assume that news service employees went into the work with their eyes open. Even so, the writers of this book always have been amazed by the number of persons they have encountered who chose to leave individual newspapers and then complained bitterly when a wire service sought to move them about.

Writing and editing.   Since all news writing involves the same purpose and the same rhetorical principles, the process of preparing a story for the wires does not differ greatly from that of preparing a story for a newspaper. What variations there are will be discussed briefly, however, because they can be troublesome at first, even psychologically.

All news writing is supposed to be concise. But AP and UPI style might be termed terse. Word saving must be *intensified* here, if all essential facts are to reach wires shared by many other bureaus.

A story may be worth a column of space in a local newspaper, but its news significance and interest outside the city may be retained in two hundred words or less for the wire. The press service writer must boil out the fat. He must also disregard detail which could be important locally but is almost valueless to readers in other cities or states.

It goes without saying that terseness will be *intensified* yet again in writing for broadcast.

The wire service writer must phrase his sentences more directly and more actively since, as we have seen, such a style is the clearest and most economical.* He will have to forego the privileges enjoyed on many newspapers whose editors favor full-blown prose and whose pages permit elaborate detail. Even on papers

* See chapter II, p. 25.

wherein space ordinarily is "tight," a reporter will encounter days when a lesser volume of advertising will allow him to let himself go. But there is no such space fluctuation on press association wires; the speed at which words may be teletyped remains constant, as does the number of minutes in the day or night.

This is why the flow of news from all bureaus must be regulated by control points. Otherwise some bureaus would never get to the wire in a twenty-four-hour period. Usually there are three control points: one for the state wire, one for the regional wire, and one for the national wire.

Even so, many schedules—brief messages describing the story being offered—are rejected daily as unwire-worthy, or a reduction in wordage is ordered, by the control points.

The foregoing applies to the bulk of the routine hard news. It does not mean that wire services never move long stories. Quite frequently a single story on a top news event will run several thousand words. This might move in one piece, if the occasion demanded, but an initial portion followed by adds is customary.

The formula is: both writer and editor are dedicated to the task of adjusting a story's length to its news significance elsewhere.

Also *intensified* in wire service procedure is the attention paid to accuracy. A single mistake is instantly multiplied to nearly two thousand errors in newspapers and as many more broadcasting stations. Any one or all of these outlets conceivably could be sued, along with the wire service, if the error were libelous and went uncorrected.

To meet this exigency news agencies make use of the "kill" and the "elimination." Either can be moved swiftly, as a bulletin. If the erroneous material is dangerous, the "kill" makes it mandatory that newspapers and broadcasters withhold the story from their audiences. The "elimination" is employed if the mistake is innocuous or if the story content is old or in poor taste. Whatever the reason, a substitute story (or portion of the story) usually follows as quickly as possible.

It is a tribute to their care that wire services rarely find it necessary to use the "kill" message.

News wires, it is interesting to note, are two-way streets. When something wrong appears in a story it is often another bureau (or a newspaper or broadcaster) that discovers the error and quickly messages the point of origin. Often, too, these sharp-eyed alerters know what the correct version should be. So, while a wire service can make four to five thousand errors at once, it also has that many potential helpmates in delivering accurate reports to the reader-listener.

No less important than accuracy is *extended* emphasis upon attribution, for the over-all protection of the news agency and the outlets it serves. The reader-listener profits by the knowledge that the story's statements of fact originated with a competent authority.

Headlines excepted, the functions of the news service editor are broader than those of the newspaper copyreader, city editor, telegraph editor, and news editor. He does the work of all of these and more. He can because he handles fewer stories in a day. Most bureaus have a day editor, a night editor, and an overnight editor. The largest bureaus also have a supervising news editor, technically responsible for all cycles.

Within his tour of duty each editor determines which local stories will be used, how long they will be, and on which wires they will move. Wire stories have to be put together so that they can be amended at any time by means of inserts, adds, sub grafs, corrections, or new leads—to cover developments during the cycle. This means that conditional material, subject to change as time passes, should be kept high in the story. Thus a new lead can be held to minimum length. The idea is to preserve as much as possible of the wordage already transmitted. This saves telegraph editors from resetting myriad lines of type, a costly and time-consuming irritation. And the shorter the new top the more transmission time it saves for the wire service.

Former newspaper reporters and copyreaders are familiar with adds, substitute paragraphs, inserts, and new leads, but in wire service bureaus the use of these adjuncts is refined to the highest degree. It is the bureau editor's job to see that his rewrite men and reporters organize stories in this flexible fashion, so that all of these devices can be employed effectively.

When a writer has redone in, say, 250 words a column-long newspaper story about the governor's weekly news conference, the wire editor will continue the rendering process until no fat remains in the sentences. He probably will file the result in full on the state wire. He may file some of it on a trunk wire if the governor said anything involving other states, but this will be an abbreviated version.

Many times a story will be updated for the state wire with a new lead and the trunk version will be amended only with an insert or an add, depending upon how far-reaching in interest and news value the latest developments may be.

Among the qualifications of the wire service editor one of the most valuable is full familiarity with the problems of the newspaper's telegraph editor. It helps, of course, if the news agency editor has worked as a telegraph editor in the past. Otherwise, this awareness can be—and should be—acquired. Without this knowledge it is quite possible for wire service editors to hinder, rather than aid, telegraph editors. A needless new top on a wire service story, based on insufficient developments, is a good example. This requires newspapers to set fresh type, perhaps rewrite a headline and possibly remake a page, all at what may be a most awkward hour. Even inserts, adds, and paragraph substitutions in a running wire story, unless they are warranted, can work a hardship on telegraph desks, although this type of supplementary material might well be ignored by papers nearing a deadline. It is harder to ignore doing something about a new lead because a paper's competitor may seize upon this small advantage and win the bulk of street sales.

In actual experience there is considerable evidence that many wire service editors are not as sensitive as they should be in anticipating the complications faced by the telegraph editors they serve.

For the wire editor the schedule is the counterpart of the headline. His stories will be competing for wire space with the stories of a hundred other bureaus and offices. It behooves him to write the best possible schedule—ten to twenty words in message form —to "sell" each story to the control point. A good story can go begging for hours if its schedule fails to reflect its importance or interest. A story offered at greater length than it is worth likewise will be kept waiting for the go-ahead signal; ultimately the control point may order its wordage reduced to keep wire traffic fluid.

Above all, schedules must be specific. It is not surprising that editors who know how to write headlines produce the best schedules in the wire services.

We have touched upon a few of the principal complexities of preparing copy for the wires. There are many others, but the foregoing should illustrate in a general way how wire service procedure differs from that of daily newspapers.

Newscasting

The newspaper story, whether it comes from a local reporter or from a wire service, is aimed at the next edition. In newscasting the deadline is *now.*

Quite often a bulletin will be broadcast thirty seconds after it appears on the wire. This is the sort of communication that killed the newspaper extra.

Writing and editing news for broadcast has become a major wire service function in recent years. Condensing stories for radio and television is a demanding task, involving a distinct rewriting technique.

Almost all radio and TV stations rely heavily upon wire services for newscasts. Larger stations augment this source by maintaining their own correspondents and local reporters. Nearly all have their own newsrooms for compiling news programs according to their own specifications.

However they are set up, broadcasters require writers and editors whose point of view is adjusted to the needs of an audience that hears and sees the delivery of news.

Two primary factors are apparent at the outset: brevity and style. News summaries usually run about six hundred words— enough for five minutes of air time. Obviously each item must be kept to minimum length if the spread of the day's news is to be covered, however lightly, in this time.

Even newscasts running ten, fifteen, thirty, or sixty minutes must reflect expert word economy.

That which was written to be read in typeface does not necessarily impress the ear. A newspaper story read aloud to an airwaves audience is not only dull but usually confusing, whatever its subject matter.

Sentences for broadcast should be phrased in lucid, conversational style. Beginning radio-TV news writers—on wire services or in stations—are urged to imagine that they are conversing with friends, and to arrange their words accordingly. The AP's handbook for broadcast writers puts it this way:

". . . Broadcast news writing requires special skills because it demands *greater compression*. It must be *terse*—but at the same time it must be *clear* and *precise*. . . .

"You cannot achieve clarity unless you keep in mind the fact that you are *writing for the ear*—not for the eye. You must train yourself to *think in terms of sound*.

"One of the best ways to determine how your copy will sound on the air is to *read it out loud*. You can't, of course, sit at your typewriter chattering like a magpie. But you can accomplish the desired results by *mouthing* the sentences you have written.

"This procedure will enable you to spot awkward phrases, involved sentences, and unclear passages." *

The Associated Press Radio-Television News Style Book, pp. 4, 5.

In one respect radio-TV news writing is almost the opposite of newspaper writing. The newspaper story and the wire service story written for newspapers offer first the most important facts (in the lead and upper paragraphs), then taper off to lesser details in the middle and final portions. The radio-TV account, on the contrary, starts narrowly and expands, to retain the listener's interest.

For example, it is best not to present the key fact in the first sentence of the item. Use a buffer sentence, in general terms, to lead the listener into the news. Instead of beginning with the statement that "John Jones was killed today . . . ," write it:

> "A Billings man was killed this morning in a two-car accident near Butte. John Jones was trapped behind the wheel for nearly . . ."

The broadcast news writer often backs into his story this way because he assumes (correctly) that some listeners are busy or are giving only token attention to the broadcast. They half-listen until an item that grabs them comes along.

Any ambiguity is certain to mislead part of the audience. If you doubt that the ear is a tricky organ, merely recall the last time you heard a friend repeat something you told him. His version very likely did not match your original.

Sentences for broadcast must remain short no matter how concisely you fill them with facts. In other words, the writer should not only be terse by using meaningful words; he should also be sparing in the number of words he assembles at one time. Short sentences are the easiest for announcers to read. They are also the easiest for listeners to comprehend.

Clarity may not be lost in a long newspaper sentence properly organized. But the same sentence would be hard to follow by ear. Unlike the reader, the listener lacks the opportunity to study the sentence again if he did not completely absorb its meaning the first time. In writing for radio and TV it is wise to limit sentence length to two lines—about twenty words.

This certainly does not provide much room for compound or complex constructions, and it is just as well. Dependent clauses are not wholly ruled out but they can present problems. The worst of these is wide separation of subject and predicate. We have already seen that such separation impedes clarity in news stories. In radio-TV news writing it actually can prove misleading.

If you write for broadcast "George Emery, son of Governor Tom Emery by his marriage to novelist Ina Fallow, died today in a fall from a mountain cliff," you can safely gamble that half your listeners will get the impression that the governor or the novelist was killed.

Here, in thumbnail form, are some tips on technique:

Keep everything—words and sentences—*simple*. Complex or rarely used words are lost upon the majority of listeners. Furthermore, they cause announcers to stumble. Most newscasters are not journalists. Odd names of persons or places need pronunciation guides.

Alliteration, the use in sequence of several words containing vowels or consonants that sound alike, finds little favor among broadcasters. Such words are, like strange names, stumbling blocks because they are not always easy to pronounce smoothly when they follow one another. Examples:

> "Pallid and pink as the palm of the flag-flower that flickers with fear of the flies as they float . . ."

Your words must be so *precise* that there is no doubt of your meaning. Remember also that some words, easily distinguishable in print, sound alike on the air. "A knotty problem" will be heard by some listeners as "a naughty problem." Homonyms—words of the same pronunciation but of different meaning, such as "bear" and "bare"—are not precise to listeners and always should be avoided.

Writers of radio-TV news copy shun *sibilants* wherever possible because of the unpleasant hissing they set up when spoken through microphones: "Seamen struck Standard Steamship Lines at six southern seaports Sunday."

For newscast purposes it is widely agreed that the most practical *tense* for newscasts is the present perfect: "A congressional committee *has eliminated* from the farm bill an amendment . . ."; "A child *has fallen* into an abandoned well . . ." Some broadcasters contend that the use of this tense eliminates the need to repeat "today" in each item.

Grammatical rules do not always apply as rigidly to broadcast news writing. It is, for instance, permissible to write: "The senator said he *will* . . . " instead of *would*. Sentences may begin with "and" or "but," disapproved by some purists in other fields of writing. Even incomplete sentences often are heard on newscasts: "A tragedy at sea today." All of these variations from the norm should be employed sparingly, however.

Euphony is pleasant to the ear. Unless there is an easy flow, a rhythm, to sentences written for broadcast, the announcer may sound like a sixth grade student reading a theme.

In radio-TV newscasts, mechanical accuracy is almost as important as factual accuracy. Be certain your copy is free of *typographical errors*. These will throw any announcer for a twenty-yard loss.

Personal pronouns, already discussed in relation to general news writing, are particularly hazardous in broadcasting. Carelessly used, "he," "she," "it" fail completely to identify the referent. Repeat the proper name.

Identification should precede the name: "Los Angeles police chief Thad Brown . . . "; "the chairman of the assembly's highway committee, Steven Smith . . . "

Direct quotes are hard to handle in newscast writing because the listener must know definitely that he is hearing a quote and not an opinion expressed by the announcer. How to advise the audience that a quote is coming proves awkward sometimes. Most announcers avoid saying "quote" and "unquote," although years ago this was the accepted technique. Today they resort to such pronouncements as "The mayor gave his view in these words"; "This is how the mayor expressed it"; ". . . what he termed as . . ."; "The mayor went on," or "The mayor continued." None of these is ideal. In general, direct quotes are avoided unless their verbatim message and the personage speaking are exceptionally impressive.

For broadcasting purposes a sentence never is started with a direct quote. The source comes first.

Inasmuch as this is a book on general writing, it is earnestly advised that those specially interested in radio-TV news writing consult one of the many excellent texts devoted exclusively to this field.

X

The Newspaperman and the Language

(The People Talk Real Good)

H. L. Mencken, who surely must be chortling in Valhalla over the renewed language controversy of the 1960s, asserted years ago that the American vernacular had displaced standard English as the mother tongue in the United States.

Mencken said English and American were separate languages, the latter more receptive to change. He added that a climate of sloppy teaching in the United States was conducive to the ascendancy of vernacular-without-rules.

The issue that piqued Mencken's curiosity blossomed again in the early 1960s with publication of *Webster's Third International Dictionary,* which included words and usages associated by many with loose or vulgar English. Its appearance raised again these questions:

Should the language conform to the way it is used by the so-called average person or by so-called proper, educated persons?

Should the newspaperman write "like the people talk" or follow the dictates of the grammarians?

Should dictionaries serve as records of the language or guides to it?

The controversy is not new. Indeed, it raged in 1800 when Noah Webster announced he was going to compile a "compendious dictionary of the English language."

Webster claimed new words had been introduced into the language and many meanings had changed. For such an assertion one newspaper branded him a "genius of ignorance . . . a writer of pseudo-philosophical nonsense." *

The newspapers wrote numerous paragraphs in the style they believed the "Merrykin Dikshunary" would countenance. Among these was a fictitious letter from a slave asking "Massa Webster" to include *hominy, possum,* and *banjo* in his "new, what-you-call-um-Book." Those words were thought to be typical of the "low" language to appear in the first Webster's dictionary.

The key elements in the litarary wrangle really haven't changed much since 1800. The principal clash still is between those who resist change and those who advocate it.

The Permissive View

The permissive philosophy toward language maintains that "correctness" simply does not exist. The people—not Dr. Johnson, Longfellow, or H. W. Fowler—determine which words become a part of the language. If a word is used, it is acceptable despite textbooks on usage.

The permissive attitude is typified by Dr. Ellsworth Barnard's remark as a visiting lecturer at Bowdoin College: "Anything is all

*See Bergen Evans, "Noah Webster Had the Same Troubles," *The New York Times Magazine,* May 13, 1962, pp. 11, 77, 79–80.

right if it fits the occasion and expresses the intended thought." *

Lexicographer Bergen Evans put it this way:

> Man's speech is a living thing; hence, it is constantly changing. Speech is organic and hence, in relation to speech, the word "correct," which one so often hears, and so often asks, is utterly meaningless.†

Television and radio have contributed significantly to the leveling process. Apparently, announcers have felt advertisements would be more effective if they used the words of that nebulous group "the common people."

Moreover, the liberal argument gains momentum when responsible officials speak extemporaneously on television. When the late President Kennedy used the term *"finalized,"* it unquestionably catapulted to a new level of acceptance. But *The New York Times* felt obligated to comment editorially:

> Mr. President, are you sure you gave the old place a thorough housecleaning after you moved in? It seems that your predecessor left a few loose words behind that you may have inadvertently picked up. When you said yesterday, "We have not finalized any plans," it sounded for all the world like a previous occupant who once said . . . "Soon my conclusions will be finalized." In any case, please be careful where you walk, because there may be some loose syntax lying about. Meanwhile, let's invite the cleaners in. They'll have the know-how to get the job finishized.

Also supporting the leveling influence are books on usage such as *A Dictionary of Contemporary American Usage* by Bergen Evans and Cornelia Evans and *Words on Paper* by Roy Copperud.

---

*The New York Times, chronicling the statement, headlined the story: "Prof Says Bum English Ain't So Bad After All."

† He continued: "If you found a mouse, and took it to a mousologist of some kind, and you said to him, 'Is this a correct mouse?' he would think you were balmy or something. He would say it is a mouse of this species, it seems to be a mouse of this age, it's a mouse of this sex, it's a mouse of this weight. . . . He could go on talking about it all day, but he can't tell you that it's a correct mouse or an incorrect mouse." (Speech before the Associated Press Managing Editors convention.)

The student of the Evanses' book will find ammunition to support English such as the following:

"He works faster than me"; "different than"; "more unique"; "Bob as well as Frank were there"; "Refer back to," etc.

A principal lesson gained from the Evanses' work is that we should write at the lowest common denominator.

In contrast to the Evanses, Roy Copperud is a practicing journalist who writes a weekly column on usage for the trade publication *Editor & Publisher*. He frequently seems to be arguing for permissiveness in language, occasionally throwing out so-called rules for the simple reason the average person no longer talks that way or never did.

Perhaps Dr. Wilfred Funk, author of *Six Weeks to Words of Power*, sums up the liberal view most skillfully. He has argued that grammar often is nothing more than pure snobbery.*

"Language has no fixed bases," says Funk. "Like everything in life, it is a process, and while purists argue, the language pattern changes."

He notes that ungrammatical expressions often are clearer and more forceful than their grammatical superiors.

If we accept the view that newsmen should write "like the people talk," we no longer would be concerned with the niceties of grammar or the demands of preciseness.

You've probably used words such as *ain't, contact* as a verb, *like* as a conjunction, and *host* as a verb. Most persons do, some infrequently. All these words—used in the above manner—appear in *Webster's Third*. The expression *ain't,* for example, is described this way:

> Though disapproved by many and more common in less educated speech, *ain't* is used orally in most parts of the U. S. by many cultivated speakers especially in the phrase "ain't I."

Or, as Will Rogers said: "Maybe ain't ain't correct, but I notice a lot of folks who ain't using ain't ain't eating."

* Wilfred Funk, "There Ain't Nothing Wrong With Ain't," *The American Weekly,* February 13, 1958, p. 31.

If *ain't* truly is used by many cultivated speakers, it would appear newspaper writers might at least consider using the term. One Midwestern university professor said it was a perfectly acceptable word—a tidbit picked up by the wire services.

Approval of such language obviously encourages a promiscuous attitude toward all words. The trend is seen clearly in the use of verbs. Some writers—including newsmen—seem to think that any word is fair game as a verb—an attitude that results in sentences such as these:

> "She had been hired to *babysit* the children."
> "Police *sirened* his car to a halt."
> "He *jetted* to Los Angeles."
> "The President *helicoptered* to the Beverly Hilton."
> "He was asked to *chairman* the committee."

Conciseness might possibly be the excuse for "the chairman *gaveled* him from the stand," but such a freak as "he *homes* in Milwaukee" is in a class with that "potshotted" peace dove cited in another chapter.

And, as one advertisement announced, "This product will not *yellow* your floors."

The field seems to be just as open regarding nouns and the addition of the suffix "wise": "timewise," "businesswise," etc.

As one book on usage notes, "There is not a noun in the language to which 'wise' cannot be added if the spirit moves one to do so." *

An advertisement on television sparked one of the most publicized—and at times amusing—debates over language. The ad claimed that "Winston tastes good like a cigarette should." Purists argued that the sentence required the conjunction *as,* not *like.* They pointed to respected texts on usage. But those in the permissive camp referred to actual usage in speech and writing dating as far back as 1579. They maintained that insistence on *as* ignores

---

*William Strunk, Jr., and E. B. White, *The Elements of Style* (New York: The Macmillan Co., 1959), p. 50. But the authors add: "The sober writer will abstain from the use of this wild syllable."

the language as it has been spoken for nearly four hundred years. One writer asserted: "You cannot say, 'Well, everybody was wrong for four hundred years and I'm right.'"

Perhaps one of the most convincing arguments for permissiveness in language—at least so far as the reporter is concerned—is that newspapers themselves have contributed significantly to the leveling trend. Look up *host* as a verb in *Webster's Third* and you will find examples from newspapers in California and Massachusetts and from a well-known quality magazine.*

Many newsmen, without a trace of a scowl, type *contact* as a verb meaning to communicate or get in touch with someone. Other writers have tried in vain to maintain the precise meaning of the verb—to touch. Authors of textbooks on usage admit that the purists are losing this battle. The Evanses, for example, state that contact is "accepted in spoken English today and probably will become the usual term in written English as well." Copperud doubts if anyone can limit the meaning of the word.†

Many facets of the liberal viewpoint toward language make sense. The language does change. The people, at least in part, determine what is acceptable at certain levels of society. The mass media have adopted many of the usages that offend the purists. Communication frequently is facilitated by using the lowest common denominator.

*Bergen Evans, in a speech before the Associated Press Managing Editors, said: "*The New York Times* wrote a very silly editorial on the appearance of the *Third Webster,* in which they stated that they were not going to use it, they were going to stick to the good old *Second Webster.* If they were, they would be out of business right now. You can't publish a newspaper in '63 or '64 with the language of 1934. . . . In their bleating, Webster pointed out that the largest single source they had drawn from was *The New York Times.* Obviously the editors don't read their own paper. Incidentally, . . . I took that issue, the issue of *The Times* in which they made this bold and lunatic announcement, and there were over 170 usages in that issue which were countenanced by the *Third Webster* which they said they wouldn't use, and were not countenanced by the *Second,* which they said they would use, and in the very editorial there were two of them."

†He adds, however, that contact as a verb has not fully emerged into the "sunshine of complete acceptance and is still partly in the shadow of its commercial origin."

The Purist View

Major arguments of the purist viewpoint seem to center on the assertion that the leveling influence is destroying the precision of the English language.

The word *enormity*, for example, long has meant *wickedness*. But it frequently is used now in place of *enormousness*. Sometimes the results are humorous, such as the charity-campaign advertisement that spoke of the "enormity of our effort." The distinction is fading; regretfully, the language is losing a precise word with a precise meaning.

Contrary to the preachings of the language levelers, the expanded use of the word *enormity* leads to confusion, not clarity. Readers who know the word link it with its original meaning. Readers who don't know it are encouraged—by the context in which they find it—to think of something enormous.

The purists decry the fact that *disinterested* and *uninterested* are being used as synonyms. A judge presumably is *disinterested* in a case; that is, he is interested in an impartial and objective manner. But he certainly is not *uninterested*—without interest.

Gilbert Highet, writing in the publication *Horizon*, has pointed out the corruption of the word *cohort*. His discussion is worth examining in full:

> Should we form a committee? appeal to Congress? take it to the United Nations? Is there any hope?
> Or has it gone too far?
> "Cohort" means a body of soldiers: a battalion or regiment, something like that. A pure Latin word, it has been in English for hundreds of years. In Milton's *Paradise Lost* God sends the archangel Michael down to expel Adam and Eve from the garden, and with him "the cohort bright/ Of watchful Cherubim."

An excellent word, it got into everybody's mind from Byron's splendid poem "The Destruction of Sennacherib." The facts are in the Bible: Second Chronicles, Chapter 32. Byron's poem begins, in galloping dactyls:

"The Assyrian came down like a wolf on the fold,
And his cohorts were gleaming in purple and gold."

That is, his regiments wore splendid uniforms, to overawe the poor Jews.

From Byron's poem the word "cohorts" probably passed through McGuffey's *Readers*. At some time within the last fifty years or so a reporter remembered this fine poetic sentence, and inserted a concealed quotation from it into a newspaper story. Who he was, and what his subject, I cannot tell; but what he wrote was something like this:

"At today's parade in honor of St. Patrick, none stepped out more bravely than Police Captain Francis X. McGeoghegan, followed by his splendid cohorts."

Now, you know what reporters are. They do not read books. They read newspapers. The word "cohorts" stuck in the mind of another reporter who read this piece. And he in his turn wrote something like this:

"Borough President Mario Attilio Squarciafico attended today's hearing at City Hall, with all his cohorts."

Next, someone else used the singular. He was the real murderer:

"One of the principal cohorts of Mayor James J. Walker during his tenure of office was . . ."

So now "cohort" has almost gone. People think it means "assistant." Or they are not quite sure what it means, but they believe it describes an individual who is somewhere nearby. Recently, I heard a charming weather forecaster on television point to her orchid and say, "I got this from a gentleman cohort." Do you think she meant "escort"?

You may say, "Wait. This is only journalism, therefore vulgar and unacceptable and scarcely worth discussing."

No. It has now entered literature. J. D. Salinger, the sensitive novella writer, has passed on to his readers the two misunderstandings of the word: one, that it refers to an individual and not a group, and the other, that it is civilian and not military. In *Raise High the Roof Beam, Carpenters* one of the brittle Glass family finds himself walking through the East Seventies with a little deafmute, nice situation, dressed for a wedding, good farce. "A silk hat materialized in the air beside me, and my special, only technically unassigned cohort grinned up at me."

Poor cohort. It means a trained body of soldiers in full uniform. But now it is being used to describe a man who gives an orchid to a girl, or a deaf-mute dwarf wearing a silk hat.

I still think it is worth saving, but who has time to picket the White House? Anyhow, the President is too busy conferring with his cohorts.*

Why worry about such distinctions? ask the modernists in speech. What difference does it make if the reader knows what you mean? The purists, generally, admit some truth in the liberal position, but not enough to overcome the disadvantages of using words loosely.

If *enormity* comes to mean *enormousness,* if *disinterested* is used interchangeably with *uninterested,* if *cohort* becomes a synonym for *companion,* what have we gained? Nothing. But we have lost valuable words with specific meanings. We have simply given up something for nothing.

The purists point out that ignorance has been the principal agent for change. A word that takes on a new meaning—such as *protagonist,*† which is regarded by many now as a synonym for *proponent*—acquires its modern definition by force of inaccurate usage. When a word is misused consistently, the dictionary compilers bow to the error. Moreover, they are yielding to error with unparalleled speed. They appear to be hurrying to embrace new meanings.

It would seem that usage by the general public should not be allowed to "establish" an error. For instance, the Evanses point out

---

*Gilbert Highet, *Horizon,* Winter 1964, Vol. VI, No. 1.

† Said H. W. Fowler in *Modern English Usage:* "Protagonist. Leading actor in a drama; hence one who takes the chief part in a play, novel, a story; but in recent use, also 'an active participant or leader'; 'leading person in contest, champion of cause.' The word has no right whatever to any of these meanings (*champion* or *advocate* or *defender*), and almost certainly owes them to the mistaking of the first syllable (representing Greek *protos,* first) for *pro,* on behalf of—a mistake made easy by the accidental resemblance to *antagonist.*"

that the name Frankenstein—used properly—is the name of the monster's creator, not the monster. But they add: "None the less the term is now established as a name for any monstrous creation, especially one that threatens to destroy its creator." When Mary Wollstonecraft Shelley invented her fictional characters, she left the monster unnamed. No matter how many persons call him Frankenstein, they still are inaccurate.

And, a misquotation, regardless of how often it is said or written, still is a misquotation. Lord Acton did not say "power corrupts," a sentence so often attributed to him. He said "power tends to corrupt." Despite the widespread use of the former expression, it still is wrong.

For years the English language has remained precise yet flexible because it maintained a successful balance between stability and change. The purists and the levelers have kept each other in check.

But in the 1960s the purists are coping with two new forces: television and educators who support a minimum standard.

Clifton Fadiman has coined the term "Televenglish" to describe the trend. Says Fadiman:

> Do not feel bad when you hear the broadcaster say he feels badly. Just remember that all men are created equally. When the friendly emcee shyly confides to his millions of listeners that he feels nauseous, do not misinterpret this as self-criticism. Applaud the Televenglish teacher who reiterates that Ford Is America's Winningest Car, who describes "gorilla" warfare, and who reports that so-and-so flew *into* Chicago today.

This difference between spoken and written language is a vital element in the argument of the purists. A speaker does not rely solely on words. He can wave his arms, shout, grimace, or bang his fist on a table. He can repeat a phrase or recast a sentence if his audience looks puzzled. But the writer—especially the newspaper writer—cannot recapture his audience. Working within time and space limitations, he must present an original version that is precise, crisp, and understandable.

Theodore M. Bernstein, who refers to the modernistic philosophy as "delinguancy"—a word he coined, then abandoned quickly —implies that at least part of the blame for a loose attitude toward language rests with teachers of English.

Who needs teachers and what is there to teach, he asks, if a major premise of instruction asserts that correctness is a relative matter depending on levels of usage.*

Others have argued similarly, citing works such as a textbook titled *The High School Curriculum*. It points out that many youngsters say "I ain't got no" because their parents say it. Furthermore, their parents see no reason why they or their children should change. The expression communicates effectively, they say, and that means it's acceptable.

Those who support the purist position also are quick to point out that a liberal attitude toward language has a snowballing effect. The permissive writer moves in one direction—more permissive. The result:

One wire service story referred to a quail hunter with an *automatic rifle* and a dog which *sighted* the birds. A city editor promptly responded: "He must be quite a shot if he hunts quail with a rifle. And a hunting dog doesn't sight quail, he detects them by scent."

A story said actress Debbie Reynolds was *munching* soup, eggs, and crackers. The sentence brought this reply: "You are OK on the crackers. Even on the soup, assuming it was consommé madrilene that got left in the freezer too long. But munch eggs! Gentlemen, you have missed a story. Get us a piece about how Debbie eats hard-boiled eggs with the shells on."

A cliché in an Eastern newspaper exploded into this absurdity: "Although identified mainly with the Yiddish Art Theatre, which he founded in 1918 and which was a mecca for Jewish theatergoers. . . ."

One account of a collision between two ships at the mouth of

*Theodore M. Bernstein, "The Problem of Delinguancy," *The Bulletin of the American Society of Newspaper Editors*, November 1, 1961, p. 1.

the Mississippi River said one was hit with a "fatal force that ripped open staterooms and crumpled one vessel *like a smashed banana.*" Terming it a "screwed-up simile," one editor said: "Now I tried to conjure up a scene on the muddy Mississippi of a ship so wrecked and twisted that it looked as if it had been in an encounter with a verbal fruit cart. The vision just didn't materalize."

In short, permissive writing has a tendency to lead to inaccurate or ludicrous prose.

Where should the newsman take his stand? If he accepts wholeheartedly the liberal view, he will, indeed, ignore the fact that the written language was designed for precision and perfection. If he becomes a purist, he may find himself opposing change when the meanings of the very tools he works with constantly are shifting.

A purist in the newsroom will find himself in as much trouble as a leveler. For example, the managing editor of the Seattle *Post-Intelligencer* decreed a few years ago that the word *victim*, because it rarely was used properly, was barred from all news copy.

Technically, a victim is a person sacrificed to some deity or a person deliberately injured or destroyed by someone else. Therefore, a pedestrian who falls into a street excavation or is inadvertently run down by a motorist is not a *victim*.

Reporters and copyreaders quickly turned to Roget's *Thesaurus*. The result prompted columnist Douglass Welch to write:

> Henceforth, you are going to read in the *Post-Intelligencer* that somebody is the "recipient" of an accident, as in "The recipients were taken to King County Hospital." Or "Seven wretches were removed from the wreckage." Or "I am," said the congressman, "the shorn lamb of one of the greatest conspiracies ever launched against an honest official."

The night city editor, asked what synonyms could be used in place of *victim*, was quoted as saying: "I don't know. It beats the hell out of me."

When the dictum resulted in several awkward leads, the managing editor—called Zeus by columnist Welch—relented and *victim* bowed to popular usage.

The possessive form supplies another example of how newspapers have accepted the general usage. In the old form, a headline would be written: "Charles's Tonsils Out." Most newspapers today would write it: "Charles' Tonsils Out." They are ignoring tradition. They have changed.

Yet, at some point, the newsman should erect at least a tentative barrier to change. Theodore Bernstein has described his job at *The New York Times* as that of keeping "a general foot on the brake and a guiding hand on the steering wheel" of change. Many editors, it would seem, harbor similar philosophies.

The most logical position for the newsman would appear to be a trifle right of center. He should be neither a stiff-necked purist clinging to rigid rules nor a soothing champion of the language spoken by the masses. He should not lose touch with either the popular tongue or the language of the educated.

Sir Ernest Gowers, the British authority on usage, put it this way in an address to the English Association in 1957: "We can rid ourselves of those grammarians' fetishes which make it more difficult to be intelligible without throwing the baby away with the bath water."

Why should the newsman remain slightly to the right? For these reasons:

(1) The purpose of the press is to communicate information accurately. In a complex space age, it cannot achieve such a goal by using vague words any more than a surgeon can operate effectively with a dull scalpel.

(2) Readers, it would seem, expect literate language in newspapers. The press is regarded by many as the last bulwark of the English language. The educated man may accept the word *ain't* in a television comedy, but he does not anticipate or approve its use in a news story.

(3) Respected newspapers and wire service bureaus do not condone loose language. Indeed, they would support the state-

ment by John Ruskin, the British author-critic, that whatever language a well-educated gentleman knows, he knows precisely.

(4) The tendency might exist to confuse the liberal viewpoint with evasion or plain laziness. A person who knows his language and his grammar and deliberately violates the so-called rules bears little resemblance to the person who doesn't know them and justifies the language in his news stories by saying he "writes like the people talk."

Index

Accuracy, 123, 144
Adjectival phrases, 86, 89
Adjectives, 81, 86–89
Adverbs, 89
Alliteration, examples of, 188
American Newspaper Guild, 35
Analogy, 95, 96
AP, 89, 93, 95, 104, 110, 114, 116,
    117, 133, 134, 135, 140, 156,
    157, 158, 159, 163
    see also Associated Press
AP Log, 152
AP Writing Campaign, 64–65
AP Writing Committee, 74
Approximation, danger of, 37
Associated Press, 110, 111, 112,
    116, 128, 138
    see also AP
Attitude of writer, 73–79

Attribution, 48–51, 104–105, 183
Auditory description, 82

Background story, 62
Baillie, Hugh, 119
Balance, in sentence, 99–100
Baldwin, Hanson W., 33
Barkley, Alben, 139
Barnard, Dr. Ellsworth, 192
Beacon Journal (Akron), 151
Benchley, Robert, 118
Berger, Meyer (Mike), 86, 90, 137
Bernstein, Theodore M., 72, 85, 103,
    201–203
Bowdoin College, 192
Boxes, 63
Brevity, 12, 121

Brighter Side, The, 67
Brites, 63

Capp, Al, 55
Christian Science Monitor, The, 115
Clarity, 12, 122
Clauses:
  conditional, 22
  dependent, 188
  poor alignment of, 16
Clichés, 36–37
Clippings, 144
Cluttered sentences, 14
Colloquialisms, 35
Colorful writing, elements of, 98
Completeness, 12
Considine, Bob, 109
Contrast, in feature lead, 95
Copperud, Roy H., 29, 145, 193, 196
Copydesk, function of, 169–172
Copy editor, 171
Copyreader, 172
Correspondent, function of, 167
CP, 118
Crowley, Ray, 39
Crozier, William P., 7
CTPS, 133

Daily News (New York), 110, 135
Dam, The, 85
Dana, Charles A., 55
Dangling modifiers, 32
Darrow, Clarence, 146
Dayton *Daily News,* 152
Dependent clauses, 188
Descriptive nouns, 68, 89
Descriptive writing, techniques of, 80
Detail:
  choice of, 15
  needless, 14
Details, attention to, 82–85
Dictionaries, 192

Dictionary of Contemporary American Usage, A, 193
Duncan, Don, 150

Editing, 66, 169–173, 181
Editor:
  copy, 171
  news service, 183–185
Editor & Publisher, 29, 145, 194
Editorializing, 87
Eliot, T. S., 100
English Association, 203
Euphony, source of, 97, 99–100, 199
Evans, Bergen, 193, 196, 199
Evans, Cornelia, 193, 196, 199
Examiner (Los Angeles), 132

Facial descriptions, 82
Facts, use of to generate impact, 81
Fadiman, Clifton, 200
Feature story, techniques of writing, 147–164
Figures of speech, 36, 92–95
Flesch, Dr. Rudolf, 55, 59
Funk, Dr. Wilfred, 194

Gallico, Paul, 85
Gardner, Erle Stanley, 33
Gibbs, Wolcott, 29
Gilmore, Eddie, 98
Gobbledegook, 38, 71
Governmentese, 38–39
Gowers, Sir Ernest, 203
Guild Reporter, The, 35

Hayakawa, S. I., 26, 81
Headlines, writing of, 171–172
Henshaw, Tom, 150
Herald Express (Los Angeles), 140
Highet, Gilbert, 197

High School Curriculum, The, 201
Hinshaw, David, 137
Homonyms, 188
Horizon, 197
Human interest story, 61, 139–143
Humor, use of in lead, 118

Imprecision, 68–69
Incompleteness, examples of, 51–53
Inform, failure to, 17
Interest, development of, 12, 58–60
International News Service, 110
Interpretive writing, 62
Inversion, 29–32

Jargon, 43–44
Journal (Lafayette), 152
Journalism schools, 5–6

Kearns, Jack (Doc), 138
Keavy, Hub, 152

Lancashire, David, 83
Language controversy
    permissive view of, 192–197
    purist view of, 198
    and newsmen, 202
Last Caprice, The, 143
Leads:
    attribution in, 104–108, 128
    definition of, 101–102
    essentials of, 120–125
    good, 120–125
    humor in, 118–120
    long, 129
    perfect, 103
    question in, 113
    quotes in, 111–113, 130
    shocker, 114
    time element in, 126–127
    words, choice of, in, 125

writing, techniques of, 101, 102,
    105–107
Legalisms, 39–42
Lewis, Joe, 143
Life, 85, 155
Li'l Abner, 55
Lindbergh, Charles, 155
Loh, Jules, 150

Maher, Charles, 95
McCormally, John, 155
McNulty, Pat, 151
Medical writing, 44
Menchin, Robert S., 143
Mencken, H. L., 137, 191
Metaphor, 92, 94
Mirror (Los Angeles), 132, 133, 134
Mirror (New York), 113
Modifiers, dangling, 76
Moody, Sid, 150
Morgan, Murray, 85
Mulligan, Hugh, 148, 150
Murder Up My Sleeve, 33

Needless detail, 14
New York Times, The, 33, 72, 85,
    90, 119, 133, 137, 154, 171,
    193, 203
New Yorker, 29
News, language of, 11
News (Hutchinson, Kans.), 155
News (New York), *see Daily News*
News story:
    essentials of, 125
    unusual angles in, 105–108
Newscasting, writing and editing
    for, 185–190
Nouns, descriptive, 68, 89

Obituaries:
    hints on writing, 144–146
    leads for, 132–136

Obituaries (cont'd)
  preparation of, 6
  techniques of writing, 131–146
O'Neil, Paul, 155
Opinion words, 87
Organization of material, 54–65

Partial quotes, 72
Participial phrasing, 32
Parts of speech, 88
Periodic sentence, definition of, 26
Personification, 95
Pett, Saul, 147
Phrases:
  adjectival, 89
  poor alignment of, 16
Possessives, forming of, 203
Post (Washington), 135
Post Intelligencer (Seattle), 160, 202
Press agents, 44
Pretentious writing, 68–70
Profiles, 62, 150
Pronoun, personal, 189
Public relations, 44
Publick Occurrences Both Forreign
  and Domestick (Boston), 131
Pulitzer, Joseph, 144
Punch line, 114–115, 149
Puns, examples of, 37–38

Question, use of in lead, 113
Quigg, Jack, 57
Quotations:
  effective use of (in lead), 111–
    114
  overuse of, 68
  unnecessary use of, 71
Quotes:
  direct, 189–190
  in feature, 158
  in lead, 130

Radio, writing and editing for, 185
Ragsdale, W. B. Jr., 150
Readability:
  elements of, 12
  roadblocks to, 13
Reader-interest, developing of, 56–
  59
Realism, 81
Redundancy, 14, 72, 86
Reporter:
  faults of, 76
  role of, 11
  writing habits of, 76–79
Repository (Canton, Ohio), 151
Rewriting, 168–169
Reynolds, Quentin, 135
Rhythm, 97
Rogers, Will, 194
Roget's Thesaurus, 202
Runyon, Damon, 67, 110
Russell, William Howard, 95

Saint-Exupéry, Antoine de, 83
Semantics, 9
Sentence structure, importance of,
  25–26, 165, 188
Shocker lead, 114
Sibilants, 188
Siddiqi, Zamir, 152
Simile, 92–93
Simple sentence, structure of, 13,
  17–18, 25
Simplified sentence, essentials of,
  18–23
Six Weeks to Word Power, 194
Stories, types of, 61
Story:
  conversational approach to, 60, 70
  elements of, 65–68
  organization of, 54–65, 184
  unconventional approach to, 65
Stull, Don, 119
Style:
  elements of, 28–53

conversational, 186
Suspended-interest, use of:
  in feature, 156–157
  in lead, 114

Talese, Gay, 154
Tartarian, Roger, 96
Taste, 67–68
Technical terms, 16, 42–45
Television, writing for, 165, 185–190
Tense and number, 23
Thurber, James, 118
Time, 29
Time, element of in lead, 126
Times (Los Angeles), 132, 133, 134, 135
Times (New York), *see New York Times*
Times (Seattle), 150
Tone, 67–68
Torgerson, Dial, 163
Tribune (Des Moines), 151
Trite expressions, 36–37
Twain, Mark, 100
Typographical errors, 189

United Press International, 88, 157

UPI, 86, 89, 134, 135, 136, 142, 156, 158, 159, 160, 173

Verb forms, misuse of, 37
Verbs:
  active, 23, 90
  colorful, 109–110
  effective use of, 90–92
  passive, 23–24
  placement in sentence, 21
  tense and number, 23

Walker, Stanley, 89, 90
Watch Your Language, 85
Webster's Third International Dictionary, 191, 196
Welch, Douglass, 160, 202
White, William Allen, 136
Whitehead, Don, 83
Wiegand, Karl von, 110
Wire editor, 184–185
Wire services, writing for, 165, 173–185
Wordiness, 13
Words:
  arrangement of, 11, 98–100
  choice of, 28, 33–35, 37, 98–100
Words on Paper, 193
Writers, faults of, 45, 73